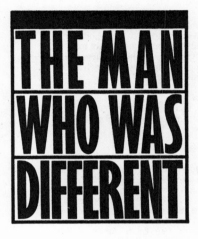

THE MAN WHO WAS DIFFERENT

GIEN KARSSEN

D1521957

NAVPRESS ◢
A MINISTRY OF THE NAVIGATORS
P.O. Box 6000, Colorado Springs, Colorado 80934

The Navigators is an international Christian organiza-
tion. Jesus Christ gave His followers the Great
Commission to go and make disciples (Matthew
28:19). The aim of The Navigators is to help fulfill
that commission by multiplying laborers for Christ in
every nation.

NavPress is the publishing ministry of The Navigators.
NavPress publications are tools to help Christians
grow. Although publications alone cannot make disciples or change lives, they can help believers learn
biblical discipleship, and apply what they learn to
their lives and ministries.

Unless otherwise identified, all Scripture quotations
in this publication are from the *Holy Bible: New
International Version* (NIV). Copyright © 1973, 1978,
1984, International Bible Society. Used by permission
of Zondervan Bible Publishers. Other versions used:
*Good News Bible: The Bible in Today's English Ver-
sion* (TEV), Copyright © 1976 by the American Bible
Society; and the *Amplified New Testament* (AMP), ©
The Lockman Foundation, 1954 and 1958.

Printed in the United States of America

*I dedicate this book
to all men and women who,
in their mutual relationships,
do not wish to be guided by tradition
or stereotyped role patterns
but want to follow the example of Jesus Christ,
the Man who was different.*

Contents

Author

Gien Karssen lives in the Netherlands. She is a Navigator representative living in The Hague, and has personally ministered to women throughout Europe for many years.

Other NavPress books by Gien Karssen:
Her Name Is Woman (Books 1 and 2)
Beside Still Waters

Acknowledgments

I extend my grateful thanks to my friends who helped realize this book: Nel Benschop; Frank and Nynke Dijkstra, Wil Doornenbal, Marieke Tichelman, Erik Veenhuizen, and George Winston, who read the manuscript and gave valuable suggestions; and Betty Froisland, who typed it.

Preface

Nearly two thousand years ago some Greek men visited the Jewish Passover in Jerusalem. These men were constantly looking over my shoulder, so to speak, as I wrote this book. Their words, "We would like to see Jesus" (John 12:20-21), continually rang in my ears, deepening my desire to look at Jesus again for myself, especially His attitude toward women. The question I asked myself was, "How did Jesus act toward women?" It seemed to me that in our modern age, with its lengthy debates about a woman's place, role, or position, this question is too seldom asked. It is necessary that He gets a voice in the matter.

Looking at Jesus' attitude toward the women of His day, who varied greatly in character, position, and way of living, became a heart-warming experience for me. As I read the Scriptures again, I met a Man who took every woman completely seriously. He recognized each woman's worth and made her aware of her own importance. He never put the female secondary to the male. Jesus even made Himself vulnerable by serving women, which was unheard of in that culture.

11

I observed this Man who was averse to prejudice, who did not use different measuring sticks. He refused to be guided by questions stemming from culture or tradition.

I was impressed by His understanding of and respect for women. It was clear that women, therefore, felt so at ease with Him.

I saw that He didn't overlook the wrongdoings of a woman who made a mess of her life. Yet He would open her eyes for new beginnings and a hopeful future.

The stories in this book are presented in a direct, personal, dramatic way. They have no theological pretension. Possibly you will visualize the circumstances of these encounters differently. There is certainly room for this.

It became very clear to me that Jesus' thoughts and actions were completely different from those of other men of His day. He, the Son of God, God Himself, stood above and outside the prejudices of His time. He likewise expects men today to follow His example in their dealings with women. His standards will never be outdated.

Men and women who accept this challenge in their mutual relationships will bring a new dimension to their lives. They will bring the fulfillment a step closer to the original plan of God from the time of Creation. And they will be a blessing to humanity.

1
He Offers a Woman His Friendship

"Jesus loved Martha and her sister and Lazarus."
(John 11:5)[1]

"Sir, we would like to see Jesus." This is the request of some foreigners to Jesus' disciples. In their land they have heard about Jesus. Now, since they are in Jerusalem, they don't want to miss the opportunity to meet Him personally. Wise people!

People who help us see Jesus in a special way are two women, Martha and Mary, and their brother, Lazarus. "Jesus loved Martha and her sister and Lazarus."

The central theme of the Bible is that God loves everyone. Jesus came to earth and gave His life because He loves every person dearly.[2] But, like any other human being, He has a need for friendship. That need is met by these three people in Bethany. Jesus is averse to the set role patterns of His time, which disapprove of friendship between a man and a woman, making it suspect.

Martha and Mary have a distinctive place in Jesus' life. This mutual affection doesn't stem from gratitude for cured diseases or forgiving of sins. It is voluntary, based on character, sympathy, and friendship. That is the meaning of the word here used for "love" in the original text.

Martha and Mary are independent women who openly

offer hospitality to a group of men. They don't hesitate to be known as friends of the Man rejected by many.

Martha is mentioned first. Probably she is the eldest. She is the hostess in the home where Jesus and His disciples can drop in unannounced and at irregular times. Jesus Himself doesn't have a home He can call His own. He has no place where He can truly relax and be at ease.[3] The best substitute is this home in Bethany.

The Middle East is known for its hospitality, but what Jesus expects of Martha and Mary can only be expected from friends. Sometimes late in the evening (they cannot give a call ahead), the group of thirteen men arrives in Bethany. After a tiring day along dusty roads there is a need to be refreshed. Beds must be organized and food prepared. There are no refrigerators or deep freezers. Bethany doesn't have a supermarket. Food has to be bought at the little markets in Jerusalem two miles away, and every single pound has to be transported by foot or on a donkey's back.

Jesus, although very sensitive to the needs of others, doesn't hesitate to cause them this trouble. They are His friends, are they not? Friends are to help one another, even if it causes inconvenience and sacrifice. Small wonder that on one such unexpected occasion Martha gets upset. Mary proves to be so captivated by Jesus' words that she sits down to listen, leaving her sister to do the work alone. This action marks the limit of Martha's patience. "Lord, don't you care that my sister has left me to do the work by myself?" she asks with irritation in her voice.

Certainly Martha for a moment loses sight of priorities, for which the Lord has to correct her. But Martha's reaction is also a proof of friendship and trust. Jesus, besides being their prominent guest, is also her friend, someone to whom she can candidly speak her mind, even though she does it critically.

Martha and Mary differ greatly in character. Martha is the active, regulating extrovert. She proves her affection by *doing* things. Mary is more introverted, eager to learn, a woman notable for her spiritual and intuitive way of living. These differences sometimes cause a clash, more so since they are sisters, of whom the eldest often tries to dominate.

Jesus has for both Martha and Mary the same warm sympathy. Both are allowed to be as they are, as God created them. Jesus cherishes both of them for who they are, the energetic Martha just as much as the contemplative Mary. Listening to Jesus' words is important, but supplying food on the table is important as well. Martha is not corrected because she takes care of this, but because, nervously, she likely does more than is needed.

Martha takes the correction seriously, but it doesn't throw her off balance. Here again she shows character. She continues to serve the Lord and the others with her domestic abilities. That is what He expects from her. The last time we meet Martha is at a dinner honoring Jesus. She serves, and Mary shows her affection in her own way—without her sister complaining this time.

Much has happened in the meantime. Lazarus becomes seriously ill. Quickly a message is sent to Jesus: "Lord, your friend is very ill." It is a mere notification, not even a request. To ask for help from the Great Physician, who has healed a countless number of people, who over and above is their friend, any more words would be redundant.

Martha and Mary, always ready to oblige Jesus, make an appeal to His friendship. They expect Jesus to come right away. But Jesus stays where He is, in Perea. When He finally arrives, Lazarus is already dead and buried.

Martha and Mary weep many hot tears during these days—not only for the loss of their only brother but also because of their disappointment about Jesus' staying away.

Nobody feels more lost than the person who feels forgotten by God. The sisters fight critical thoughts toward the Master in their own hearts, but they also read these same thoughts in the eyes of those who offer their condolences. "He opened the eyes of the blind man. Could He not have prevented Lazarus from dying as well?"

As in the situation of Job, the purpose of this suffering is hidden from the sisters' perception. The fact that Jesus has stayed away stems not from His lack of concern but from His obedience to God, His Father. Through this suffering, God wants to glorify His Son and make people believe in Him.

The joy yet to come will more than equal their depth of sorrow. Lazarus' resurrection from the dead will be a far greater miracle than his healing could have been. His resurrection surpasses the two Jesus performed elsewhere. Lazarus didn't die just a moment before (like Jairus' daughter), nor was he on his way to the grave (like the widow's son of Nain).[4] With Lazarus, decomposition has already started!

When Martha hears that Jesus is approaching, she doesn't remain at home sulking about the apparent negligence. Her active nature doesn't deny itself. She goes out to meet Him.

"If you had been here, Lazarus would not have died." There is honest reproof in her voice, but the direct approach is also a proof of friendship. Martha doesn't feel inhibited to tell Jesus precisely what she thinks. The relationship between them is one of openness and dialogue. And she has faith: "But I know that even now God will give you whatever you ask."

To a woman, a Samaritan, Jesus tells who He is: the Messiah, the Savior of the world. Here, again to a woman, He describes to Martha two other aspects of His identity: "I am the resurrection and the life." To people who believe, this spells assurance of a blessed, eternal life after death. "He who believes in me will live, even though he dies; and whoever lives and believes in me will never die."

Most people fear death and face it stoically. But Jesus declares that death has been boldly abolished and changed "from a door that closes into one that goes open for everyone who knocks."[5]

"I am the resurrection and the life. He who believes in me will live." These words, which for twenty centuries have given comfort and perspective to Christians at funerals and which still appear on death announcements, are first said to Martha. Few words have given more encouragement to those who mourn.

Again Jesus talks with a woman about who He is. Remarkably, that woman is the domestic, energetic Martha, not the seemingly more spiritual Mary. What an encouragement for those women who, when comparing themselves with the two sisters, conclude that they are more like Martha, although they would rather be more like Mary. Here again Jesus is the Man who is different, who doesn't think in stereotypes but who judges according to the heart.

Not that all this is clear right away to Martha. What is going on is too great and far-reaching to be comprehended instantly. This slowness to understand surrounds Lazarus' resurrection.

Increasingly it dawns on Martha how Jesus identifies Himself with their sorrow, how the death of His friend makes Him angry and sad at the same time, how it moves Him to tears and to a holy indignation over the power of sin, which is the root cause of death.

Jesus didn't forget His friends in their time of need. On the contrary, in coming He endangered His own life. The threats around the area of Jerusalem are so fierce that it takes a real effort to get His disciples to accompany Him. They warn Him persistently that a journey to Jerusalem will mean certain death.

Lazarus' resurrection causes many people to believe in

Jesus. The greatest result of the miracle is not that a man returns from his physical death but that many people receive new and eternal life. As Jesus predicted, this honors God, and that's what it's all about.

All this makes some people so bitter that they take steps to kill Jesus. During the brief time before Jesus' death, His freedom is virtually gone. With His disciples, He travels to a region near the desert. This, also, is the price Jesus pays for His friendship.

We often think that God prevents people who love Him from suffering. But this is not true. Jesus allows even His friends to experience deep sorrow. And when they remain faithful to Him, He rewards them abundantly in every way with more than they could possibly expect!

NOTES: 1. Read Luke 10:38-42, John 11, and John 12:1-11.
       2. John 3:16
       3. Luke 9:58
       4. See Chapters 5 and 8.
       5. Malcolm Muggeridge, *Jesus* (Ambobook/Baarn, 1976), page 97

QUESTIONS FOR PERSONAL OR GROUP STUDY

1. "What does the word 'friendship' bring to your mind?" In answer to this question, more than a hundred men and women from twelve countries listed the following words, in this order: acceptance, honesty, reliability, openness, feeling relaxed. Are these the kind of words you would list? Would you name other things, or list them in a different order?

2. How do you see these characteristics taking place between Jesus and Martha?

3. What remarkable facts do we read about Abraham and Moses? (Exodus 33:11, James 2:23). How do these facts strike you?

4. Jesus mentions the word "friends" three times in John 15:13-15. How does He prove His friendship? What does He expect from His disciples?

5. What is Jesus saying about friendship in the parable in Luke 11:5-8?

6. Jesus didn't limit His friendship to people of a certain group or social class. How can you apply His attitude in your own life?

7. What friendship do you experience in your relationship with God and with people around you?

2
He Takes a Woman's Side

"I tell you the truth, wherever the gospel is preached throughout the world, what she has done will also be told, in memory of her."

(Mark 14:9)[1]

Only a few of her words have been preserved for us. Yet she is one of the best-known women in the history of Christendom. Mary of Bethany doesn't make a name for herself by her salient pronouncements but by her godly attitude and warmth of character. In the home with her sister Martha and brother Lazarus, she occupies her own place.

Next to the always busy, practical Martha, Mary seems somewhat phlegmatic, but that is only the way it looks on the surface. Tradition has colored the sisters in a somewhat biased way. When we look closer, we see that Mary is not the passive woman many people think she is. In her own way she is a radical—someone who knows what she wants, which is not always accepted gratefully by others.

Mary understands Jesus probably better than anyone else. The repeated visits of Jesus and His disciples, sometimes staying overnight, verify this.

We meet Mary, like Martha, three times. The first time is when Jesus pays them an unexpected visit. Luke registers the occasion soberly, placing the so-called active-domestic and the passive-contemplative sisters next to one another.

An initial glance at Luke 10:40 may seem to indicate that Mary shuns her responsibilities on that occasion, which rubs Martha in the wrong way. A proper reading of the text shows, however, that Mary initially plays her part, only to seat herself later with the disciples at Jesus' feet. (Does she perhaps think that Martha makes too much fuss?) What she does is courageous.

In this Jewish culture, women belong in the kitchen. Their responsibilities are purely domestic. In this way Martha meets the expectations. But a woman sitting among men at a rabbi's feet is unheard of and just not done. Only boys are instructed in the Law. For girls this is unbecoming. Instruction in the Law for women is, according to the rabbis, "to cast pearls before swine." Among the plagues of the world, the Talmud lists "a virgin who wastes her time in prayers."² Israel's religious leaders purposely keep women ignorant, and so curtail their spiritual development. According to most rabbis, women just don't have enough sense to understand these things.

Mary knows all this. She also knows that she, a woman, is a spiritual being who, just like a man, cannot live by bread alone. Therefore she takes this unusual initiative, sitting among the men at Jesus' feet. Jesus' presence frees her from the feeling of guilt for being interested in something other than typical female affairs. Our modern age has words for her attitude, such as being progressive, liberated, and assertive. Without even trying, Mary becomes a pioneer. She considers herself simply a common woman with a hunger after the things of God, someone who doesn't want to miss possibilities that lie within reach.

Mary proves that she knows Jesus well. He doesn't blame her for breaking through existing role patterns. He even takes her side against Martha. His reaction is more generous than she probably expects. He praises her. "Mary has chosen what is better, and it will not be taken away from her." What the disciples think or say on this occasion we don't read.

After Lazarus' death, the difference of character in the sisters is again apparent in the way they react to sorrow. It seems to paralyze Mary; Martha remains active. Jesus deals with each according to her personality. Martha receives the incredible honor of being told deep spiritual truths the Lord so far has told no one. And seeing Mary's sorrow moves Jesus so deeply that it brings Him to tears.

Nobody notices it when Martha goes outside to meet Jesus. As the head of the family, she apparently receives personal notice of His arrival. Perhaps she is in the kitchen at the time, preparing refreshments for the many people who come to offer their condolences.

Mary's feelings evoke responses from others. When the people see her distress, they want to comfort. When they expect her to visit the grave to weep, they follow her.

When Mary meets Jesus, she says literally what Martha said earlier: "Lord, if you had been here, my brother would not have died." This is what the sisters have repeatedly said to each other in the past days.

The dreadfulness of what has happened seems to strike Jesus that moment in full force. He feels the horror of death through the loss of one of His truly good friends. He empathizes with the heartache of the sisters who, with their brother gone, now also miss the status of having a man in the house.

Jesus probably realizes that His friends are also disappointed in Him. He did not meet their expectations. That is hard for the Man who will sacrifice His life for His friends and for His enemies, but who still has to explain His delay.

Jesus is no stoic. He doesn't think, "Men don't cry." Along with Mary and before the eyes of many guests, Jesus shows His feelings openly. He weeps.

The final meeting between Jesus and Mary is right before His death, when the sisters receive Him as the guest of honor at a dinner. This becomes His farewell to them, but Mary is the only one who has a foreboding of this.

The family is well off. The spacious house that can lodge so many houseguests at a time and the copious meals prove this. The sisters are held in respect with the Jews in Jerusalem. All of this shows that they belong to the nobility.

But Jesus doesn't choose people according to influence or wealth. He doesn't classify according to social status. He is a friend of the poor—this He proves convincingly—but He doesn't exclude the rich. Here in Bethany it is the higher social class that supports Him so that He can serve the poor freely.

This explains the costly perfume Mary bought. The money she puts down for it—a year's wages for a laborer—could easily be used to feed five thousand people.[3] But the hospitality of the home in Bethany proves that the poor around them lack for nothing. Mary knows that the Law requests them to give to the poor liberally and joyfully. God has allowed the poor to remain in Israel in order to test the generosity of the rich. It may be that she and her family are blessed with earthly goods because they have kept this commandment, and so they experience the blessing God promises His people.[4]

But today something else is going on. Mary knows intuitively that this is the last time she can do something for Jesus. Happily she doesn't suppress this impulse, for such an omission could never be remedied.

Single Mary doesn't have a child to offer to the Lord as did Hannah and Elizabeth. But she has personal resources: she has money. Therefore she spends this enormous amount on Him. Love doesn't look for excuses for what it cannot give. Nor does love think in terms of money. Love is creative. It finds ways of expression. Jesus rightly says she does what she can. More He doesn't expect; less is an insult.

At the outset of Jesus' life, a rich man from the East paid Him homage with a gift of myrrh. Now, at the close of His life, Mary honors Him with her precious balm. It is the tribute offered to a king. Later it will serve to embalm Jesus' body. Then it is to honor the dead; now it is to honor the living Lord.

Upon entering a home a guest in Israel always gets some drops of perfume placed on his forehead. Mary spends an entire jar on Jesus. She doesn't empty this jar drop-by-drop as is usually done with perfume. She breaks the jar and lets the precious, fragrant oil flow liberally. Jesus no doubt recognizes in the broken jar the symbol of death. Jews used to have the broken jar buried with the corpse. "She poured perfume on my body beforehand to prepare for my burial."

Mary is so captivated by her Lord that she forgets that an honorable woman should keep her hair up in company of others. But in Jesus' presence one doesn't think of such trivialities! She lets the perfume flow liberally over Jesus' head until it drips down on His feet. Then she dries His feet with her loosened hair.

The fragrance permeates the entire house. It stays in Jesus' hair and saturates His clothes. Some days later at the Cross, when the Romans divide His clothes among themselves, they take that fragrance home with them. Hanging on the Cross, the aroma in His hair reminds Jesus of what Mary did. Few things arouse memories as does a fragrance. The sweet smell of her hair reminds Mary for a long time to come of that last meeting.

After twenty centuries, this fragrance still lingers in the world. Every time new Bibles are translated or printed, the truth of Jesus' words are discharged again. "I tell you the truth, wherever the gospel is preached throughout the world, what she has done will also be told, in memory of her."

It is sad that one of the loveliest events in the life of Jesus is tarnished by criticism. Judas quickly seizes the opportunity

to make Mary suspect. Accusing Mary of squandering money,
he protests loudly and bitterly. He claims that she should have
given the money it cost for this perfumed oil to the poor.
Judas is the treasurer of the group. Dishonest as he is, he
reacts hypocritically. It is a sour reaction for a man who has
been Jesus' discontented disciple for three years. Spending
this amount out of love for Jesus is, in Judas' words, a waste of
money. Right after this, he moves out to betray Jesus for a
handful of silver coins.

Even more painful than the criticism of Judas is the
reaction of the other disciples. They, too, are indignant about
Mary's action. They disapprove of the way she has spent her
money. These men have regularly enjoyed her hospitality.
They have often sat at her table. They never uttered one word
of protest on those occasions when Martha outdid herself to
take the best possible care of them. No one talked about the
poor then.

Mary is a woman Jesus thinks highly of. He stood up for
her before and praised her desire to learn. The disciples saw
how Jesus sorrowed for her and with her at Lazarus' death. But
it carries no weight with them now. They haven't learned
from experience. They've gathered no insight into Jesus'
thoughts regarding women.

The disciples' criticism is painful for the sensitive Mary—
both for her and for the Lord, to whom the reactions are even
more obnoxious. She doesn't defend herself. But Jesus de-
fends her. He takes Mary's side. Again! With the fragrance of
perfume in her hair, these are the last memories she has of the
Lord.

NOTES: 1. Read Mark 14:3-11, Luke 10:38-42, John 11, and John 12:1-8.
2. William Barclay, *Corinthians* (1982), page 136
3. John 6:5-10
4. Deuteronomy 15:10-11

QUESTIONS FOR PERSONAL OR GROUP STUDY

1. Mary experienced criticism for the way she exercised her faith, even from "religious" people. What can a follower of Christ expect from an unbelieving world? (John 15:18-21, 16:33).

2. What was Jesus' own experience, and in what ways can this stimulate and encourage us? (Matthew 16:21, Hebrews 12:3).

3. Read Hebrews 4:15-16 and 5:8, and then summarize your thoughts from these verses.

4. What encouragement do you read in Isaiah 63:9?

5. Read Mark 14:9, and describe the potential result of adversity in our lives. How does this relate to Romans 8:28?

3
He Chooses to Be Vulnerable

"When a Samaritan woman came to draw water, Jesus said to her, 'Will you give me a drink?'"
                                                    (John 4:7)[1]

More than anything else, Jesus needs rest. He and His disciples have just completed a long trip. At midday, it is very hot. Jesus doesn't walk another mile with His disciples to the city of Sychar to buy food. He remains behind at the well alone. The well is situated in an open field.

Scarcely has He seated Himself when a woman of the city comes to fetch water. Strange. Sychar has its own well. This woman, however, doesn't want to face her fellow citizens. Thus she fetches her daily ration of water far from home, and at a time when no sensible person puts up with unnecessary strain. Women usually fetch their water in the early evening when it is cooler, making it *the* outing of the day.

Jesus has every valid excuse to pay no attention to her. No rabbi speaks openly with a woman on the street. That is beneath the dignity of a religious teacher. Moreover, Jews despise Samaritans. They have not forgotten that the Samaritans assimilated with the Gentile nations, thus giving up the purity of the Jewish race. Jews don't take the Samaritans seriously. They do their utmost to prevent contact with them. A Jew traveling from Judea to Galilee, or vice versa, gladly makes the long detour through the country to the east of the Jordan. He takes a trip twice as long as necessary just to prevent going through Samaria.

Jesus shows no surprise about meeting the woman at such an unusual hour. Although at this moment rest is more welcome than a talk in the burning midday sun, He asks for a drink. It is a remarkable request. Jews and Samaritans keep strictly separate drinking utensils. Most Jews wouldn't think of drinking water from a jar touched by a Samaritan. Nor does Jesus need human help to lessen His thirst. There are millions of angels at His disposal. Just as He recently changed water into wine, He can easily supply Himself with water now. But personal interests and thoughts about reputation are always secondary with Jesus, especially when He sees a person in need. For such people He came into the world. So it is now. It doesn't become clear if He receives the water He asks for.

Other recorded talks of Jesus with women take place either in an intimate circle or in a crowd. This conversation takes place openly at a crossroads and at a well, a place where people meet. Every passerby can observe that Jesus is talking with this woman. For her sake He makes Himself vulnerable in almost every way.

It is one of Jesus' longest conversations recorded. In spite of this, it is still a condensation of what is being said. Barclay compares this with the minutes of a meeting: only the main points are mentioned.

The atmosphere is striking. Nothing indicates that Jesus treats this woman with any less respect than He treated Nicodemus, an honored Pharisee He met earlier. Here we even find a personal interest and warmth missing in Jesus' remarks with Nicodemus. It is a conversation in which the woman's maturity and human dignity are sustained and her input taken seriously.

The woman gives no sign of the slightest inhibition

regarding the normal taboos of this kind of unexpected encounter. She seems at ease, and responds sincerely and frankly. Here is a man who treats her not just as a woman but as an individual. The condescension for her womanhood with which many men approach her is absent. She senses no haughtiness or criticism, and this disarms her.

Yet she remains on guard. There is either suspicion or mere curiosity in her voice when she answers Jesus' request for water. How come a Jew, a man at that, is asking a favor of a Samaritan woman?

Jesus doesn't respond to her question about their social and religious differences. He didn't come to strengthen prejudices but to solve them. The woman thinks of what separates; Jesus thinks of what unites.

Jesus gently steers the conversation in the direction of spiritual things. He approaches her directly and personally when He says, "If you knew the gift of God and who it is that asks you for a drink, you would have asked him and he would have given you living water."

Living water reminds Jews of thirst for God. The well-spring of living water, according to their prophet Jeremiah, is the Lord Himself.[2] Hadn't David said, "For with you is the fountain of life"?[3] The Jews know from Scripture that the thirst of a soul for God is like a deer panting for water.[4] They are aware of the invitation of Isaiah: "Come, all you who are thirsty, come to the waters."[5] As the people of God, they count on the promise, "I will pour water on the thirsty land, and streams on the dry ground; I will pour out my Spirit. . . ."[6]

But this woman doesn't seem to understand the double meaning of Jesus' words. All she wants is for her basic need for water to be satisfied. It would be wonderful if from now on this daily trip could be forgotten. Fetching water has become a trauma for her. With every step toward the distant Jacob's well, she judges herself. She even sees this judgment confirmed in the eyes of the people around her.

The Samaritans have only the Pentateuch, the five books of Moses. This small portion of the Bible, however, is enough for her to know that God has created man and woman to be monogamous; adultery is sin. Being aware of this, the Samaritan woman places herself outside the community. She is an outcast, and she knows it. This awareness comes not just from the outside; it is her conviction inside.

Her life is dominated by eroticism and sexuality. She has had five husbands. How often she was either married and rejected or became a widow is not clear. Marrying so often is not considered to be proper, and living together with a man who is not hers is against God's Law.

Living water to her is well water. Critically, she asks herself, "Can this man validate his promise? This well is more than a hundred feet deep. He would have to be an extraordinary man to bring water up without a bucket. Even our forefather Jacob, who gave us this spring, could not do such a feat."

The woman has a ready tongue, saying candidly what she thinks. She can formulate her thoughts clearly and has the courage to express them to a man. In her culture this is unusual.

Here is a woman completely at ease in Jesus' presence, who dares to be herself. Nowhere do we see that the Lord disapproves of or reproves such frank behavior. Nowhere do we observe the slightest irritation or room for the thought, "How does a woman get it into her head to talk to *Me* in *such* a way?" Jesus always meets women with sincere interest and respect. For that reason alone, every woman should welcome Him in her heart!

The conversation that develops now is on a high level. The Lord clearly shows the direction, but He doesn't force her in any way. He considers the woman intelligent enough to draw her own conclusions. Their talk has now clearly come on double track. Jesus refers to water that gives eternal life; the woman wants water that makes the trip to the well redundant. The roles are also reversed. Instead of asking, Jesus has become the Giver. Now it is she who asks for water.

A climax is drawing near. John 4:4 indicates that Jesus _had_ to go through Samaria. The encounter at the well shows that this woman is His reason. She must be freed from her emptiness and lack of perspective. She needs to get to know Jesus as her personal Savior. Then a new future will open up for her. Being blessed herself, she will become a blessing to others. But this she doesn't know yet.

So far Jesus hasn't revealed to anyone who He really is. He has kept this from His own family, His disciples, and even from the theologian Nicodemus. The first person who will hear from His own lips that He is the Messiah, the Christ, is this Samaritan woman. According to the social and religious standards of the Jews, she is least qualified. She is a woman, she doesn't belong to His own people, and she is not of blameless behavior. Jesus again chooses to be vulnerable.

This morning she left her home as usual, not knowing what the day might bring. When she returns home later, her life will have changed drastically. But first an obstacle has to be cleared away. She cannot receive the wonderful gift God has in store for her until she has confessed her sins.

Jesus tells her, "Go, call your husband and come back."

Those words touch her deeper than a convincing lecture about morality and sexuality could ever do. In an objective way they expose the crumbling foundations of her life.

Since there is no reproach, she needs no defense. The woman understands that Jesus leaves only one possible answer to her: "I have no husband."

But instead of rebuke or condemnation she hears words of openness and insight: "You are right when you say you have no husband. The fact is, you have had five husbands, and the man you now have is not your husband."

The woman has seen right away that this is no common Jew. Now she discovers that He is a prophet of God. She understands from Jesus' reaction that He knows her life story, and that He also knows why and where things went wrong in her relationships with men.

Better than anyone else, Jesus is aware of the anguish and the sorrow this woman has experienced over and over again. He does not excuse the men and their part in her situation.

To be known through and through is a sobering experience, but also a liberating one. For a moment the woman seems to want to steer the conversation in safer channels with some quick questions about religion. She points to its forms: where do we have to worship, here or in Jerusalem? Behind her questioning Jesus detects a desire for God. He sees a woman who, in spite of everything, thinks about God.

Worshiping God, He says, is a matter of the heart, not of the place of worship. "God is spirit, and his worshipers must worship in spirit and in truth."

For a woman whose contact with men was mostly in the sexual realm, it is refreshing for her to have a man discuss spiritual matters with her. It is communication in depth, something she is in great need of. Now she can share her deepest thoughts. She expresses her conviction concerning the Messiah, who is coming. She says that He will explain everything.

These are remarkable words for someone who doesn't know the scrolls of the Prophets and the Psalms. She believes that the salvation brought by Christ, the Redeemer, will not be restricted to the Jewish people. "He will explain everything to *us.*" This is a significant spiritual insight. Few people have expressed themselves so clearly about the Christ.

Then she hears the words she will never forget as long as she lives: "I who speak to you am he."

Recently at the Passover Feast in Jerusalem many people started to believe in Jesus' name. Yet He didn't entrust Himself to them, "for he knew all men. . . . He knew what was in a man."[7] But the Lord makes an exception in this case. This woman may know who He is. To this woman, who in no way belongs to a privileged group, He reveals Himself without hesitation. According to race, sex, and behavior she doesn't meet the requirements, but she is not beyond the reach of Jesus' searching love. In order to win her, Jesus chooses to be vulnerable, as a man and as a Jew.

She may be the first person to know the identity of the Savior. This meeting has a liberating effect, vertically in her relationship with God and horizontally in its outworking with people. We will see this effect clearly in the next chapter.

NOTES: 1. Read John 4:1-26.
          2. Jeremiah 17:13
          3. Psalm 36:9
          4. Psalm 42:1-2
          5. Isaiah 55:1
          6. Isaiah 44:3
          7. John 2:24-25

QUESTIONS FOR PERSONAL OR GROUP STUDY

1. Jesus informed the Samaritan woman that He was the Messiah. In the following references Jesus also refers to Himself by saying "I am. . . ." As you read these passages, discover what personal characteristics He presents, and note briefly what each one means to you (John 6:35, 8:12, 8:58, 10:36, 11:25, 14:6, Revelation 1:8,17-18).

2. Read and meditate on Philippians 2:6-11. Describe in your own words how vulnerable Jesus made Himself and to what purpose.

3. What strikes you most about Jesus' vulnerability?

4
He Draws Out the Best in a Woman

"Many of the Samaritans from that town believed in him because of the woman's testimony, 'He told me everything I ever did.'"

(John 4:39)[1]

When the conversation between Jesus and the Samaritan woman is at its peak, the disciples return with their food. They are stupefied to find the Master talking with a Samaritan, especially a woman.

These disciples are men of their time and tradition. Feelings of contempt toward the Samaritans were sucked in with their mother's milk. It is quite something for them to travel with Jesus through Samaria. That they shop in a Samaritan town and are willing to come into personal contact with its people shows that they are grasping that Jesus' commission surpasses prejudiced Jewish thinking. But that His message extends itself to women is unheard of. That the gospel of Jesus Christ is universal, surpassing not only boundaries of nationalities but also those of sectarianism and the sexes, is beyond their comprehension.

The serious faces of Jesus and the woman reveal that they are taken up in very deep thoughts. That is even a greater riddle. The rabbis teach that women are not capable of receiving religious instruction. They also say that a long conversation with a woman is detrimental to a man and a sign of forsaking the Law. According to rabbinical standards, Jesus here tramples underfoot the laws of tradition and decent behavior.

The serious atmosphere around the Lord and the woman keeps the disciples from asking questions, but the woman reads their disapproval in their eyes. She feels doubly rejected, maybe even more because she is a woman than because she is a Samaritan. The way the men look at her hurts. Jesus draws out the best in her; they do the opposite. She now begins to realize that she has indeed met a man who is totally different: the Christ. He has also made her see herself in a spiritual mirror.

These are the two most important discoveries a person can make. This woman has now discovered how Jesus is all-knowing, all-wise, just, understanding, and full of love. In this light her life is a hopeless and sinful mess. But this one encounter puts her life on a completely new track. The full impact of this new life she will understand only gradually, but the fact that everything has changed and is becoming new is proven right away.

Her need for water is forgotten. She leaves the jar where it is. A new vitality takes possession of her. There is a spark in her eyes and a streak of determination about her mouth. Quickly she returns to the city. She must share her happiness.

Jesus lets her go. Another man in the same situation wouldn't like to be announced by a woman, and certainly not by this one. But Jesus takes that risk. He has confidence in her.

The inner freedom of the Samaritan woman is so radical that she harbors no desire to escape her fellow citizens. On the contrary, she accosts them. It is senseless to cover up her past. Her fear of people and their criticism has left her anyway, because Jesus, the Messiah, accepted her!

This is a bold woman, who calls a spade a spade. "Come, see a man who told me everything I ever did," she urges. With

keen discernment, she understands that there is no better way
to arouse interest in Jesus than by telling what He did for her.

People see the joy on the face of a person who is set free.
Could this be the woman they saw heading for the well,
self-engrossed and dissipated only a few hours ago? He who
can change such a battered, closed-in life so suddenly and
radically must be an exceptional person!

All of a sudden the road from Sychar to the well becomes
scattered with people. Jesus and His disciples see them coming from afar. Their long white gowns, bathed by the sun,
shimmer in the summer breeze. The people of Sychar meet
Jesus and become personally convinced of who He is. The
woman is right. He is the Savior of the world! This recognition
that Jesus' own people have so far withheld from Him, He
now receives from these despised Samaritans.

The woman begins to understand what the spring of
water that Jesus mentioned is all about. The slumbering
desire for God that Jesus detected in her becomes a fountain
of living water within her, one that can quench the thirst of
many others. That stream will grow deeper and the river bed
will grow wider, heralding the work of the Holy Spirit, who
soon will take possession of God's people in all His fullness.[2]
Samaria will be the first area, after Jerusalem, where the Holy
Spirit will be poured out. The conversion of the Samaritan
woman will bring forth permanent fruit.

The woman nobody wanted to associate with, whom all
had written off, becomes the first evangelist outside the
borders of the Jewish land. The encounter with Jesus
becomes for her and many others a life-renewing experience.
Faith in Christ cleanses her from a stained past. From now on
people will speak about her gratefully. She moves into history
as a messenger of peace and happiness. She finds her own
place in society with her own identity and a new awareness of
self-worth. She becomes a living proof that Jesus Christ can

renew a life completely. Instead of being despised, she becomes a representative of encouragement and hope.

This encounter also marks a turning point for women in history. At the time that this happens the position of women is sad. The Jews are influenced in their thinking by the nations around them, not by God's thoughts about women. The Greek dramatist Euripides, for one, estimated the value of ten thousand women to be less than that of one single man! The Mishnah, the book of Jewish oral law, was a little more positive, but still figured one hundred females to two males. The Jewish historian Flavius Josephus judged a woman in every way inferior to a man. Involuntarily the words of author J. van der Hoeven come to mind: "What in the world did we men do that we were so over-estimated?"[3]

Jesus doesn't come with contradicting pronouncements, which would not be understood and would work in the wrong way. But His consistent attitude underscores the fact that He considers women completely equal with men. He places one woman together with one man. At His coming in the world women receive equal place.

This we see right after Jesus is born. When He is presented to the Lord in the Temple, there are Simeon and Anna, a man and a woman, to greet the Child. It is Anna who takes the initiative to tell the good news in Jerusalem right away.[4]

Jesus illustrates His speeches with examples of both men and women. In the synagogue of Nazareth He refers successively to the widow in Zarephath and Naaman the Syrian.[5] His first healings concern also a man and a woman: the demon-possessed man in the synagogue of Capernaum and Simon's mother-in-law.[6] In His parables He places a man, who lost one of his hundred sheep, and a woman, who misses one of her ten silver coins, next to one another.[7] And these are not the only examples.

The conversation with the Samaritan woman follows the

one with Nicodemus, a man of power in the Sanhedrin. These conversations complement each other. The one with Nicodemus stands out because of its intellectual and theological content. It reveals the need for being born again. The conversation with the woman illustrates the change in her life that sprouts from the new birth, and the positive results this can have on one's surroundings. Both men and women are thus instrumental in showing what is needed for accepting and spreading the gospel.

John is the only Gospel writer who records Jesus' meeting with the woman of Samaria. This encounter made such an indelible impression on him that some sixty years after the event, every detail is still fresh in his mind. He again experiences that hot noonday in the reviled country of Samaria. The conversation, the questions and answers from one to the other, are so deeply engraved in his mind that he remembers them clearly.

Usually the Samaritan woman is judged harshly when she is talked about. The wrongdoings of her life are placed under a magnifying glass, and question marks are superimposed on her openness on spiritual matters. It was a diversion to cover up for herself, we say.

Jesus shows us how a self-sacrificing approach that doesn't condemn or camouflage wrong can draw out the best in a person. It has surely changed a lost life to a source of blessing for many.

NOTES: 1. Read John 4:27-42.
  2. John 7:37-39
  3. *Squint-eyed Little Angel* (author's translation) (Amsterdam, The Netherlands: Publ. Ploegsma, 1971), page 40
  4. Luke 2:22-38
  5. Luke 4:25-27
  6. Luke 4:33-39
  7. Luke 15:3-10

QUESTIONS FOR PERSONAL OR GROUP STUDY

1. Many Samaritans came to believe that Jesus is the Savior of the world. Their interest was aroused by the words of the woman. What made her message so convincing? (John 4:39-42).

2. What happened to Zacchaeus after he met Jesus? (Luke 19:1-9). What comparison do you see between Zacchaeus and the woman of Samaria?

3. Study the following accounts of Paul's life before and after meeting Jesus Christ. Describe who he was before and after that meeting (Acts 22:3-15, 1 Corinthians 15:9-10, Philippians 3:4-9, 1 Timothy 1:12-15).

4. What convinced the Jewish Council of the genuineness of the words of Peter and John? (Acts 4:12-13).

5. By what is the authenticity of our faith measured? (1 Corinthians 4:19-20).

6. Try now to summarize these meetings with Jesus in the context of 2 Corinthians 5:17.

5
He Feels Personally Involved

"When the Lord saw her, his heart went out to her and he said, 'Don't cry.'"

(Luke 7:13)[1]

Slowly she walks behind the bier. In front of her go the hired flute players and the mourning women who, according to their profession, cry out loudly. Round about her are the men and women of the city who move forward in separate groups. People feel shocked and show sympathy for this widow who is going to bury her only son. All work has stopped.

Her home lies desolate with tables and couches turned upside-down as a sign of mourning. Later, after the funeral, she will fully understand how great and pronounced her loss really is. So far there has been little time to acquaint herself with her grief. Yesterday her son was still alive, but now his body is ready for burial. In order to maintain health regulations and prevent the uncleanness that comes from touching a corpse, funerals in Israel always take place right away.

This woman is barely conscious of what is happening around her. Like any widow who is again confronted by death, her thoughts move back to the day her husband died. Memories of that painful occasion come naturally to mind.

When a Jewish woman's husband dies, she loses her safe

43

future. Along with the waifs and foreigners, she then has no rights, no secure source of income. She is left entirely at the mercy of others. As a result, widows sometimes even become prostitutes.

When a man leaves no children behind, his inheritance, according to the Jewish law, goes to his brothers or the male relatives on his father's side. A childless widow usually returns to her parents or is given in marriage to a brother-in-law. This obligatory, so-called levirate law was given to perpetuate the deceased man's name, not to provide for the widow's emotional and financial needs.[2]

Although God gave His people rules for widows, they are in fact still painfully subjects of charity. A widow, for instance, is allowed to glean ears of grain that remain behind in the fields and pick what remains on the trees after harvesting.[3] A portion of certain tithing that the people offer to God also brings some relief.[4]

Yet there are people in Israel who ignore these laws completely and enrich themselves at the expense of widows. Some people enlarge their own property subtly by moving the boundary stones that separate pieces of land to the disadvantage of a widow. Although the Lord has repeatedly warned against these practices, they continue to occur.[5]

Even spiritual leaders fail to give a good example. Instead of living according to God's laws and making other people do the same, many take advantage of the widows. Jesus judges them fiercely: "They take advantage of widows and rob them of their homes, and then make a show of saying long prayers. Their punishment will be all the worse!"[6] (The word here used for "homes" also applies to other property and possessions.) The Pharisees appropriate these laws deceitfully for their own use. Pharisees who have no mind to work give the impression that it is the duty of widows to support them financially, an act rewarded by God. Impressed by the seeming piety of the Pharisees, the widows sacrifice for them unduly.

Spiritual leaders who boast about knowing the Law to its minutest detail bitterly neglect to show this devotion in daily practice.[7] Pharisees purposely keep widows ignorant. They consider it better to burn the words of Scripture (among which are many promises for widows) than to teach them to women.

Jesus is totally different. In His eyes a woman is fully qualified for the scriptural support. He ascribes her full rights, whether she is unmarried or a widow.

This mourning widow so far has known few cares. Her only son, whom she is now going to bury, took upon himself the responsibilities of his deceased father, according to Jewish custom. He was her provider and protector. Now he is gone, and this means a double loss. Added to her grief over his death, her hope for future support is also gone. Small wonder that the Bible speaks about the loss of an only child with intense sadness, especially when it concerns the son of a widow.[8]

The procession slowly approaches the town gate. The town of Nain stands up on a hill, and can be entered and exited only through this gate. At the moment the funeral procession arrives, another crowd from below climbs up from the plain.

Jesus and His disciples have completed a day's journey from Capernaum. Many people have joined them as well. Their procession of Life comes upon this procession of death just outside the gate. This is destined to be a disastrous encounter for death!

Funerals are a daily sight in Israel. Jesus meets them often. This is the only time we read of that He comes in between. The tears of this mother touch Him deeply, even more than the fact that a youth is snatched away through death as such. Better than anyone else, Jesus understands the extent of her grief. He knows of the joy that welcomed the birth of this boy, and how carefully he was raised. He understands that the worth of a woman in the East is measured by the number of her children, especially sons. Sons mean status and prestige. Sons are insurance against old age. Do you have children? Sons? This is still one of the first questions a woman in this part of the world is asked in the twentieth century.

Does this widow remind Jesus of His own mother who (as is commonly accepted) for some time has also been a widow? Do the tears of this woman remind Him of the sorrow of His mother, Mary, when her husband, Joseph, died?

Jesus knows of the loneliness of a widow. He knows the bitter experience of a woman who, with the death of her husband, sees that her circle of friends diminishes drastically at the same time. Only other women come to visit the widow. The men normally opt out of that task. A woman who has always thought she was respected for herself often discovers that she was considered important only as the extension of her husband. Widows still experience this as an utterly painful insult to their self-esteem.

Jesus experienced this kind of sadness from close quarters. After Joseph died He also took the responsibilities upon Himself and supported His mother. Dutifully, Jesus continues to accomplish this task to the end. His last care before His death concerns His mother.[9]

Unlike the corrupt Jewish leaders, Jesus does not neglect God's instructions concerning widows. Here also He obeys the will of God. He reveals Himself as the Son of Him who sustains the widows,[10] who says, "Your widows too can trust in me."[11]

He now stands eye to eye with the mother. "Don't cry," He says. There is deep emotion in His voice. At the resurrection of Lazarus, when Jesus sees Martha and Mary weeping, He cannot hold back His tears. Jesus feels personally involved with the grief of people who suffer. He is the promised Redeemer of whom was prophesied, "In all their distress he too was distressed, and the angel of his presence saved them. In his love and mercy he redeemed them; he lifted them up and carried them all the days of old."[12]

Jesus approaches the bier. He touches it and says, "Young man, I say to you, get up!" (According to Eastern custom the body lies not in a coffin but in a kind of wicker basket, wrapped in linen cloth with a napkin over his face.) The bystanders are filled with awe as they see the dead man slowly sit up and begin to talk.

"Jesus gave him back to his mother." The mother's welfare—this is Jesus' concern. Her tears He wants to dry. Just like the prophet Elijah in his time, Jesus resuscitates the son of a widow to comfort his mother. The Lord does not overlook a widow's grief. He feels personally involved.

The calling of this young man will not be like that of another one who was called to move about the country with Jesus.[13] Jesus does not work according to set forms or methods. He approaches each individual in a personal way. Each receives his own specific task. Being at home, caring for his mother, is the way for this young man to follow Christ. The woman recovers her son, and with this she also recovers her place in society.

For the people present, this resurrection is a sign. They remember the prophets Elijah and Elisha of old and the miracles they did. "God has come to help his people," they say. Again we have a prophet in the land! Praise to God and gratitude for the miracle become the talk of the day. Throughout a wide area people talk about it. The transformed sorrow of one person becomes the joy of many.

Jesus' blessed work on earth has barely begun. He will raise others from the dead—the daughter of Jairus and Lazarus of Bethany. The first to be raised, however, is the son of an anonymous widow.

Jesus concerns Himself with this woman's unhappy lot, even though she doesn't ask for it. The returning of her son from death does not depend on her faith. Not one word is mentioned about her faith. Jesus helps because He cannot bear the sorrow of this woman. He makes a heart that is heavy with burdens begin to sing again. Because He feels involved. Because He has a special soft spot in His heart for widows. And this has not changed, even to this day!

NOTES: 1. Read Luke 7:11-17.
           2. Deuteronomy 25:5-10
           3. Deuteronomy 24:19-21
           4. Deuteronomy 26:12
           5. Proverbs 15:25, 22:28, 23:10
           6. Mark 12:40 (TEV)
           7. Matthew 23:23
           8. Zechariah 12:10
           9. John 19:26-27
          10. Psalm 146:9
          11. Jeremiah 49:11
          12. Isaiah 63:9
          13. Luke 18:18-25

QUESTIONS FOR PERSONAL OR GROUP STUDY

1. Why do you think God calls Himself "a father of the fatherless" and "a defender of widows"? (Psalm 68:5-6). For what other group of people does He care? Although Isaiah (54:1-6) speaks symbolically, what comfort can single and deserted women draw from his words?

2. To what treatment are widows apparently often exposed? (Exodus 22:22-24, Deuteronomy 16:11, Jeremiah 22:3-5, Acts 6:1). (Although these references point only to widows, we may include other unattached women in our study based on what we saw under question 1.)

3. What result does this treatment have on our personal lives and on society in general?

4. By what standard does God measure the purity of our religion? (Jeremiah 7:5-7, James 1:27).

5. We meet some other widows in Scripture. Write down your thoughts briefly for each one of them (Mark 12:41-44, Luke 2:36-38, 4:25-26, 18:1-8). How did they serve Jesus? Why did He set them as examples?

6. In light of these scriptural accounts, do you think widows receive enough attention in our society? What can be done to follow Jesus' example more closely?

7. Are there widows among your friends? What is your attitude toward them?

6
He Approaches a Woman Without Prejudice

"Jesus said to the woman, 'Your faith has saved you; go in peace.'"

(Luke 7:50)[1]

If everything Jesus did was recorded to the minutest detail, the world itself would be too small to contain all the books. This is John's conclusion at the end of his Gospel. However, we would have liked more information about the woman we meet here, the sinner who anoints Jesus' feet. All kinds of questions confront us.

Where does she meet Jesus for the first time and what takes place? Does she see Him at a distance in a crowd or is there a personal encounter? Is she present when Jesus resurrects the son of a widow in Nain? Does that possibly help her to see who He is and consequently to recognize that her way of living is on the wrong track?

One thing is certain: meeting Jesus makes her change her life and arouses a desire within her for virtuous living. The piety and faultlessness Jesus radiates reveals to her, the woman known by all in the city as a common prostitute, that she has strayed from the purpose for which she was created. She understands little of the image of God—the high responsibility for woman to be responsible along with man for the earth and its inhabitants. Instead of being a blessing, her influence has been demoralizing and destructive. But this will change. She has met Jesus!

What precisely takes place, how her faith is aroused, will not be revealed until the books of her life are opened.[2] Until then we have to be satisfied with the brief record that only Luke gives. (Because of the significant difference in place, time, and circumstances, this story should not be mistaken for the one of the anointing by Mary of Bethany.[3])

This woman hears that Simon the Pharisee has invited Jesus for a meal. Pharisees are strict orthodox Jews who take pride in a punctual observance of the Law. Generally speaking the Pharisees are not favorably inclined toward Jesus. Too often the Lord exposes them because they study the Law closely but fail to observe it in love. Instead of serving people, they try to domineer them.

Why Simon invites the Lord we can only guess. Does he want to charge Jesus with something that could be used against Him? Is it curiosity? Does Simon merely want to get better acquainted with Jesus? Or is he sincerely interested in the Man who, by His spectacular healings and miracles, is receiving increasing popularity?

Whatever the case, Simon doesn't treat his special guest with much respect. On the contrary, the reception is remarkably cool and nonchalant.

A guest entering the house of a prominent Jew could normally expect three things. The host first places his hand on the guest's shoulder and gives him a kiss of peace. This token of respect in the case of a distinguished rabbi is never omitted.

Also, after walking in open sandals on the dirt roads, a guest should always have cool water poured over his feet. Then a pinch of sweet-smelling incense or a drop of attar of roses is placed on his head. Good manners demand that these things never be neglected. By "forgetting" all three of them,

Simon was grossly violating the code of Eastern hospitality.

When a rabbi is the guest of a prominent Jew, all kinds of people can freely come in and listen to the words of the honored teacher. That is why this woman, undoubtedly against Simon's wishes, can enter undisturbed. Simon cannot prevent this.

It is standard procedure for the guests to recline at the table. Resting on the left elbow, a person lies on a low couch with his feet, unshod, stretching behind him. This explains how the woman is able to stand behind Jesus' feet.

It takes courage for this woman to appear in this gathering of people. Everyone knows that she is a woman of low morals. She feels the critics thinking, "There goes the woman who makes sin her profession."

Anointing somebody's feet as a token of paying homage, or kissing the feet of honored rabbis, is no rare custom in Jesus' time. But this woman does both with dedication, not taking the custom for granted on this special occasion. She probably plans at first to do her work quickly and inconspicuously. But after arriving in Jesus' presence she is overcome by her emotions. Tears of repentance mix with tears of joy because the Lord does not reject her tribute and gratitude. Impulsively and spontaneously she unloosens her hair and dries His feet, which become wet from her tears. This is a touching but most uncommon gesture. After her wedding day, a Jewish woman never appears with loosened hair in public. This is considered improper. But it doesn't occur to this woman. She forgets herself and her surroundings, for there is only one person who deserves her attention, and that is Jesus!

This is one of the rare moments during Jesus' earthly life when someone spontaneously and lovingly does something for *Him*. Here is someone who is thinking of Him, who wants to bring joy to Him, who wants to *give*.

Jesus and the woman so far have not exchanged a word. Simon watches it all, becoming increasingly annoyed. As a teacher of the Law, he is not touched by seeing a sinner who repents. To him, she is an incorrigibly bad woman, past correction. But Simon criticizes Jesus instead. This rabbi cannot possibly be the prophet some people think He is, for then He would know that this woman is a notorious sinner with whom no decent man can associate.

Simon is wrong. There is more than a prophet under his roof. Jesus, who reads minds as easily as words, answers Simon's unspoken question. He doesn't reprimand but talks in such a way that should lead Simon to examine himself. Although Simon openly affronts Jesus with his nonchalant reception, the Lord still loves him. He wants to win Simon. Just like the woman Simon looks down upon, he himself needs a personal encounter with the Savior—an inner touch. Simon's sins, though less spectacular, also need to be acknowledged, confessed, and forgiven. A chance is given to Simon, just as it is given to the woman.

The story of the two men who are indebted to a money lender may not seem to be relevant at first, but Jesus uses it to build a bridge to the present situation. He turns to the woman, but, sensitive enough not to embarrass her since she is deeply moved, He directs His question to Simon the Pharisee. "Do you see this woman?" Of course Simon sees her. He sees her with the eyes of prejudice. To him she is just an unfortunate case. He also sees her with the eyes of a man who is ill at ease in her presence. To him she is both attractive and repulsive. It is difficult to find the proper attitude in her presence. She is disturbing.

"He saw her better than we do. We see her through the glasses of many generations of reputable exegetes who are responsible for the tone of the respectable title given to this story: 'Jesus Anointed by a Sinful Woman.' [There is an alliteration in some languages for the words 'sinful' and 'anointed,' suggesting a sense of softness. The sharp edges of these words are long gone. They may be typical words of the Bible, but not of the visible world of today. They have a solemn sound, but we cannot visualize them very well.] After all those ages Jesus also has to ask us, 'Do you see this woman?' We only see her when we take this story out of the cotton wool of the outmoded terminology and open ourselves up to the shattering facts by giving it a new title: 'Jesus Caressed by a Whore.'"[4]

Her touch doesn't embarrass Jesus. His attitude is neutral, yet involved. He sees this woman not as an object but as a person who is observing herself in a mirror and who is then so shocked by the result that she wants to start a radically new life. For the first time in her life, a man does not speak in a condescending way about her, although Jesus does openly expose and judge her behavior. But this approach of loving confrontation actually liberates her.

Jesus doesn't excuse what she did. He speaks candidly about her "many sins." But she is accepted because she is sorry for them. He is the only one who approaches her with understanding and without prejudice. He understands how she came to her immoral behavior and how lonely it has made her. Better than anyone else, He knows how it feels to be an outcast in society.

Jesus doesn't forget the men who used her sexually, either. Here they remain out of the picture, but to Him they are equally guilty. Jesus judges impartially. He is opposed to a double standard.

Jesus then reveals the contrast between Simon's formal coolness and this woman's great love. The washing of feet that Simon omitted, the kiss he withheld, the anointing with oil he "forgot," the respect that Simon just didn't have, are all demonstrated to the Lord by this woman in a way that far surpasses the usual feet-washing ritual. This woman puts her heart into what she does. Her tears, her constant kissing of Jesus' feet, the fragrance of the perfume that still lingers in the room, are many sincere tokens of her intense love and gratitude. Her actions demonstrate that she knows she has done wrong, and also that she has been forgiven. Her demonstration of love stands in proportion to her feelings of guilt. Simon doesn't feel any guilt and consequently has little need to express love or gratitude.

Simon is pleased with himself. But his encounter with Jesus does not lead to soul-searching and repentance. Therefore he is the most pitiable of the two, because for him there is no forgiveness. Only confessed sins and admitted guilt can be forgiven by Christ.

Do the other guests realize that this woman puts Simon and all the rest of them to shame? Do they see that Simon, with all his prejudices, passes his own judgment? Do they heed the warning? They cannot know that they have arrived at the most crucial point of history, where from now on a different standard will be the rule. Jesus recognizes no real difference between a notorious sinful woman and a self-righteous Pharisee. They are both sinners who were created by God. He approaches both without prejudice. He comes to liberate one like the other from the past.

Jesus now addresses the woman for the first time directly. "Your sins are forgiven," He says.

This leads the fellow guests to say, "Who is this who even forgives sins?" Are they becoming convinced of Jesus' mission, or are they skeptical, ready to accuse Him of being blasphemous? It is not clear.

Jesus doesn't react to this. He sees only the woman. "Your faith has saved you; go in peace." These words close the door to her sinful past forever and disclose the way to a promising new future.

Her faith saves her from the judgment she has brought upon herself by her sins. She was unacceptable in the sight of a holy God, not because she was a whore, but because she was a rebellious, fallen human being. Sin estranged her from Him. Like every individual, she needed a major repair in her relationship with Him.[5]

How tremendously high is the price for peace between God and man. This fact is emphasized later when Jesus sacrifices His life, dying on a cross on the hill of Calvary just outside Jerusalem.[6]

Then He says, "Go in peace": *Shalom.* This is the farewell that present-day Jews still use to greet one another. But it is much more. Actually Jesus is saying, "Go into peace." He presents peace as something like a home in which she can live, as something surrounding her on all sides. From now on, this peace should penetrate her mind and inspire her thoughts so that she can face absolutely any situation with a sense of equanimity and confidence.[7]

Her peace with God is now restored. But peace with men still has to be won. Her place in society she will have to retrieve step by step. Sin, like an octopus that has put its tentacles around her, will not easily give up its prey. Her "clientele" will not take no for an answer without a certain amount of protest. They will try everything possible to draw her back into her former life.

Strikingly, Jesus doesn't depart from her with the warning, "Leave your life of sin." With these words He takes leave of another woman, but not this one.[8] Does He, who reads a person's heart like an open book, see that her new sense of disgust for sin and her conversion are so sincere that she doesn't need such a strong exhortation?

The peace that Jesus gives her means not only rest and quiet but also reparation and prosperity. How this prosperity is eventually worked out in her life remains hidden. But one

thing is certain: The Lord who started a good work in her will
see to it that this is also accomplished.

NOTES: 1. Read Luke 7:36-50.
        2. Revelation 20:12
        3. John 12:1-8
        4. Okke Jager, *Opklaring* (author's translation) (Ede, The Nether-
           lands: Zomer & Keuning, 1981), page 79
        5. Romans 3:23-24
        6. Romans 5:1,8
        7. Philippians 4:6-7
        8. John 8:11

QUESTIONS FOR PERSONAL OR GROUP STUDY

1. Jesus told this woman, "Your faith has saved you." Summarize from the following verses what faith is and what it does: Romans 5:1, Galatians 2:20, Ephesians 2:8, Hebrews 11:1.

2. Read Hebrews 11 and note what faith can accomplish in human lives.

3. Jesus asked Simon, "Do you see this woman?"
   a. Think about this Pharisee, his background and his attitude (see also questions 1-3 at the end of Chapter 10). How do you think he saw this woman?
   b. How did Jesus see her?
   c. Try to place yourself in this woman's shoes. Write down how you think she felt.

4. Which prejudices still seem to confront men and women in our day, and what can be done about them?

7
He Accepts Women in His Team

"Jesus traveled about from one town and village to another, proclaiming the good news of the kingdom of God. The Twelve were with him, and also some women who had been cured of evil spirits and diseases: Mary (called Magdalene) from whom seven demons had come out; Joanna the wife of Cuza, the manager of Herod's household; Susanna; and many others. These women were helping to support them out of their own means."

(Luke 8:1-3)

Which of the women first gets the idea of attaching herself to Jesus and His team? Is it Mary Magdalene? Her name is mentioned first.

Jesus has been extremely kind to Mary Magdalene. He cast seven demons out of her. This was such a drastic change that for the rest of her life she leads the way for others in following Christ. But Mary Magdalene is not the only one.

There is Joanna, whose husband occupies a prominent position at the court of Herod Antipas. Joanna lives close to two extremely lewd women: Herod's wife Herodias and her daughter Salome, who together had John the Baptist killed in cold blood. How is Joanna able to hold her own in such a corrupt atmosphere? What has the Lord done for her to make her leave the otherwise comfortable court life and become His follower? All we know is that He has healed her.

A woman in this culture is considered to be the possession of her husband. She doesn't move about independently. Is Joanna's decision to follow Christ a source of friction between her and her husband? Or does Cuza gladly allow his wife to follow the desire of her heart? Legend has it that Cuza at some point loses his position as the manager of Herod's household because of the conversion of his wife to Christ and her bold witness to the other members of the royal household.

Another woman who is healed by Jesus and who therefore decides to serve Him is Susanna. Her name, which means white lily, is mentioned only once. Does her name reveal something about her purity of character? What a privilege for a woman like Susanna, who is anonymous in her own day, to be still known through the testimony of the Bible many centuries after her death!

A well-known woman of the time is another woman named Salome, who is the mother of Jesus' disciples John and James. She is the wife of Zebedee, owner of a fishing business with employed servants. He and his family are known in the more sophisticated circles of Israel.

Salome's sons left their father's business to become some of the first followers of Jesus. She joins them later. It is generally accepted that Salome is the sister of Jesus' mother.[1] This makes her the aunt of Jesus. While many reject the Lord and others follow Him critically, Salome believes that He is the future King of Israel.

A certain ambition is not foreign to Salome. She desires for her sons nothing less than the best places in Jesus' future Kingdom.[2] Does she claim special rights because of the family relationship? Because of her social background, Salome, like Joanna, adds status to the team of people around Jesus, who for many is the despised Man of Nazareth.

Many other women travel with Jesus and His team on His last trip from Galilee to Jerusalem. They remain anonymous. One other name is mentioned: Mary, the mother of James and Joseph, the wife of Alphaeus, or Clopas. Her son James (nicknamed "the little" or "the younger") belongs to Jesus' twelve chosen disciples, along with Salome's sons. Again we meet a woman who temporarily leaves her husband and the security of hearth and home to dedicate herself to Jesus and His disciples.

Rabbis who go teaching through the countryside accompanied by their followers are in these days a common sight. Unusual here is that Jesus allows women in His team. These women are not chosen by name, like the disciples, nor are they sent to preach, to heal the sick, and to cast out devils. Yet their function in the whole setup is more distinctive than meets the eye at first glance.

Jesus' attitude toward women is exceptional. First of all, it is unusual in contrast to the attitude of the religious leaders of Israel, who are prejudiced and negative in their judgment of women. Jesus sees this over and over. His awareness of the critical thinking about women in the surrounding countries makes His attitude even more remarkable.

Among the Greeks the lot of women is truly sad. To a married woman every influence outside the home is denied. Women's quarters even have their own guards, who keep careful watch so that they can go outside only if escorted. Typical is the pronouncement of a friend of Plato: "The female sex is used to living hidden, in the dark. . . ."[3]

The Romans do not esteem women highly either. Listen to what a contemporary of Horace says: "It is easier to drain the sea or to pluck with one's own hand the stars from heaven than to keep our women from sinning."[4]

Buddhism considers woman the root of all evil. A few sayings of Buddha: "She has a two-fingers-wide mind." "Impenetrable and deep like the way of a fish in the water is the nature of a woman. She is a shrewd, sly thief, by whom the truth is far to find."[5]

How vastly different is Jesus of Nazareth's thinking. His long and intelligent conversations with women have been recorded for all to see.

"So if the Son sets you free, you will be free indeed."[6]

These words sound like music, especially in the ears of women. Christ frees a woman twice: from sin and from the stigma attached by society to her womanhood.

Every woman understands Dorothy Sayers when she writes, "Perhaps it is no wonder that the women were first at the Cradle and last at the Cross. They had never known a man like this Man—there never has been such another."[7]

So Jesus travels with a group of men *and* women, from Galilee, through Phoenicia and the East of Jordan territory, then on to Jerusalem. It becomes a trip that takes over a year. Such a journey is a silent statement in itself.

Galilee, where the women join up with Jesus, is one of the great crossroads of the ancient world. Palestine is the bridge between Europe and Africa along which all road traffic goes. Consequently, Greeks, Romans, Egyptians, and Asians all witness the example of this rabbi of Nazareth who shows how men should really treat women. Jesus doesn't treat women like things, which is often how they are treated in our twentieth-century society. (Note the advertisements in the press and on television.) Women function properly when they are involved in Jesus' life and work.

This function reveals itself in different aspects. Obviously there is the financial side. Jesus has left His carpenter job, thus giving up His source of income. In doing so He has made Himself financially dependent on the generosity of others. The Son of God—God Himself, the Creator of heaven and earth to whom everything belongs—humbles Himself in this area to the utmost.

The financial help of these women provides for an obvious need. Daily meals must be prepared for thirteen men, plus all the others who join in with the group. Clothes have to be washed and mended. Shopping has to be done. Although some of the women seem to have husbands who are financially well off, their way of spending money still depends on personal choice. Money spent on Jesus and His team is at the expense of personal purchases, the buying of nice clothes and accessories. Every woman enjoys such luxuries, but especially the Jewish woman.

The dedication of these women reaches far beyond financial help. It encourages Jesus emotionally. While many turn away and others criticize Him, here is a group that is loyal to Him. This kind of support helps alleviate discouragement and loneliness.

Luke writes that these women are "helping to support" Jesus and the twelve disciples "out of their own means." The original text uses the word *diakoneō* here, which means giving practical Christian service, something that requires the input of the total person.

Jesus understands better than anyone else the extent of the sacrifice these women are making. He knows how traveling day after day through the open country challenges their endurance. Along with Him, they face the extremes of heat and cold, and the uncertainty of accommodations for each coming night. It is risky to cast in your lot with the Man who doesn't even have a stone on which to place His head. This goes for men, but even more so for women.

Jesus also takes certain risks by accepting women on His team. Peter Ketter states, "This the scribes never did. They considered having female disciples around to be incompatible with the dignity of a rabbi. But the fact that Christ allowed women to be near Him openly declared that He valued women in a different way than they did. Christ returned to woman her complete personality as a human being. This influenced women to break with the manners and customs rooted in the overestimation of the male and the prejudice against the nature of a woman.

"Despite the constant jealousy and merciless insinuation on the part of Jesus' enemies, the fact that there is never any hint of gossip regarding His relationship with women is another proof of Jesus' sublime character, the absolute purity of His intentions, and His blameless conduct."[8]

Remarkable also is that we don't hear one single negative remark about these women. We never read that Jesus scolds or corrects them as He did His men. There is not a word among the women about strife concerning prerogatives, which among the disciples flares up highly. And these women don't take pride in the fact that they followed Jesus without pursuing personal interests. They do not expect reward, contrary to what is recorded about Peter, James, and John.[9]

Although the men, for obvious reasons, move more to the foreground than the women, the Lord doesn't exclude the female gender from His spiritual ministry. The Resurrection gives proof of this, when the angels say to the women, "He is not here; he has risen! Remember how he told you, while he was still with you in Galilee."[10] Then the women do remember, for they were present when Jesus spoke about His departure. He didn't reserve this important knowledge for men only. He taught men and women together.

We have no pronouncements from Jesus about the equality of woman to man. His teaching on this subject is shown in His deeds, which are totally convincing.

Jesus allows women to share in His physical and emotional needs. They see Him weep. He doesn't hide His feelings from them when He is tired or disappointed. On the other side, they also share His happiness and rejoice in the miracles He does. The women experience the full range of His emotions as they function in Jesus' life and work. As they experience His recognition and respect, they are encouraged and strengthened to keep going.

At Jesus' crucifixion, when all the disciples except John fail to turn up, these women followers don't leave Him. Although Jesus' suffering is unbearable to watch, yet they stay and encourage the Lord with their presence. The women remain faithful to their Lord until His death. They are also present at His burial.

Jesus takes women seriously. This is proven over and again. He listens to them. He considers conversations with them worthwhile. Jesus understands how a woman wants to be treated. He knows that she functions best when she can carry responsibility. From the time of Creation, God has given that calling to her. He therefore expects much *of* her.

The Swiss physician and counselor Paul Tournier writes in this respect, "It seems to me that if men understood women better they would expect more of them, and if they expected more of them they would promote them to positions of greater responsibility."[11] Jesus is a primary example of recognition of excellence and value in *all* people.

The women who follow Jesus bring a sense of warmth to the male existence of Jesus and His men. Nowhere do we read that the women measure themselves alongside the disciples. With typical female intuition, they add what is lacking in the male company: personal attention, care, and sensitivity. Something of the purpose of God in Creation they thus bring to expression. Society functions best and most harmoniously when it is built up by men and women together. If the female influence is curtailed, then society turns lean. It suffers when female creativity doesn't blossom, when her specific contributions are not called upon. This is the problem of Jesus' time, but not of that time alone. We still meet up often with such an unnatural limitation of human resources.

The disciples can observe Jesus' attitude toward women daily. Do they understand what happens before their very eyes? Do they really understand the new dimension Jesus has added to the male-female relationship? The answer seems to be negative.

Three of the Gospel writers—John, Matthew, and Mark (Mark writes Peter's story)—cover the role of these women in extremely brief reports, all focused on their part at the end of Jesus' life. Only Luke, always noted for being specially attentive to women, places them next to the disciples and at the beginning of his Gospel. Paul is not present with Jesus during His ministry, yet he apparently understands His message quite well. When Paul enumerates his colaborers (Romans 16), one-third of them prove to be women. He gives a circumstantial account on how much some of them meant to him personally and to his ministry.

Someone who studied this subject of the part women should play in service to Christ is the Christian physician and author Paul Tournier. In his book *The Gift of Feeling*, he emphasizes that God's plan for male and female to carry out His commission in the family, Church, and society has little materialized thus far. He states that woman's special gifts of mind and heart and the influence she can have, since she is much more person-minded than man, have been little utilized. Tournier proposes that woman's greater intuition and sensitivity, meant to be complementary to male thinking, has been insufficiently used.

Our age reaps the bitter fruit of this imbalance. Woman has been "awakened," unfortunately, more as a result of hurt emotions and underrating of her human dignity than by the inspiring attitude of Jesus Christ. This gets many women on the barricades. Others feel insecure and frustrated. Due to the course of events, men, who have had a hard time keeping up with the developments, feel insulted and threatened.

Have we who love the Lord and know the Bible, both men and women, tried to apply what we see in Jesus' example? Men and women together need to look at Jesus Christ in a new and objective way, to leave traditions of prejudice behind and together find new ways. We should let ourselves be informed, inspired, and encouraged by the One who created us. He holds the blueprint for both man and woman that will show us how to function to the optimum.

Dee Jepsen, who for some time was a special assistant to President Ronald Reagan for public liaison to women's organizations, writes, "Amazing things could happen if we [women] were recognized for our equal value, as human beings, and recognized for the contributions we make to the entire fabric of our society—in the home, the professions, the marketplace, the community, politics, education, and on and on. And as the men in our lives recognized our true value, they would begin to look at us differently. Attitudes *could* be affected."[12]

When this kind of change is eventually brought into practice, something will happen that mankind has never seen before. Then the developments that were started two thousand years ago by the Man who was different will be set into dynamic motion.

NOTES: 1. Read Matthew 27:56, Mark 15:40-41, 16:1-2, and John 19:25.
        2. Matthew 20:20-21
        3. Peter Ketter, *Christ and Women* (author's translation) (Hilversum, The Netherlands: N.V. Paul Brand's, 1937), page 25
        4. Ketter, page 37
        5. Ketter, page 53
        6. John 8:36
        7. Dorothy Sayers, *Are Women Human?* (Grand Rapids: Eerdmans, 1974), page 47
        8. Ketter, pages 308-309
        9. Matthew 19:27, Mark 10:35-37
       10. Luke 24:6
       11. Paul Tournier, *The Gift of Feeling* (London: SCM Press Ltd., 1982), page 57
       12. Dee Jepsen, *Women: Beyond Equal Rights* (Waco, Texas: Word Books, 1984), pages 48-49

QUESTIONS FOR PERSONAL OR GROUP STUDY

1. Read Romans 16:1-16. List the names of all Paul's female coworkers and describe, whenever possible, how they served him. What strikes you about their service?

2. What is your answer to the question stated in 1 Corinthians 9:5?

3. In what ways did the following women offer their share in the ministry of the gospel: Dorcas (Acts 9:36-42), Mary, the mother of John Mark (Acts 12:12-17), and Lydia (Acts 16:14-15,40)?

4. It seems that female missionaries are often getting more room to colabor independently with men than women do in their home situations. Why do you think this is true, and what do you think of this?

5. Do you think that the colaborship of men and women in the Church and in Christian organizations follows the example Jesus gave? What changes are desirable? What can you do to function best within the limits set for you?

8
He Takes Every Woman Seriously

"Just then a man named Jairus, a ruler of the synagogue, came and fell at Jesus' feet, pleading with him to come to his house because his only daughter, a girl of about twelve, was dying."

(Luke 8:41-42)[1]

Jairus is not used to going around with hat in hand asking favors. He is an influential man who normally extends favors himself. Being a ruler of the synagogue, he is held in high regard—one of the most respected persons in the community. Jairus is the administrative head of the synagogue, chairman of the board of elders, and responsible for the management of the religious services.

Jairus is on his way to Jesus, and that is far from easy for him. He is well aware of the negative attitude many people around him have toward this popular, miracle-working rabbi. Whatever prejudice Jairus might feel toward Jesus he now has to put aside. He also has to forget his dignity, for he is in great need: his child, his only daughter, is dying. The doctors apparently have given up all hope. Only a miracle can save her.

Necessity leads people to pray. Necessity also induces courage. Even though Israel's religious leaders will not support Jairus' decision to go to Jesus for help, he doesn't just quietly send a servant. Despite the adverse consequences for his career, Jairus travels openly to see Jesus. He is part of a

69

group of Jews who are growing increasingly hostile toward Jesus. Is he perhaps also afraid that Jesus will not receive him? If so, his fears are baseless.

He finds Jesus among a grateful crowd, for He is back in the country again. The Lord has just returned from the other side of the lake. In the area of the Gerasenes, He performed an enormous miracle. Although Jesus is deeply involved in a conversation with His disciples, right away Jairus receives His full attention.

Jairus kneels deeply before Jesus. His head touches the ground. It is a token of deep respect.

The anxiety in the eyes of this father reminds Jesus of the concern He once witnessed in His own parents when He had been missing as a boy. Just like Jairus' daughter, Jesus was twelve years old at that time. Twelve years of age is a crucial time for a girl in Israel. She stands at the brink of womanhood. At that age many girls are already engaged to be married.

Israel's religious leaders are far from being woman-friendly. This is another point of concern for Jairus. Girls don't score high in his land. "Hail those whose children are boys, woe unto them whose children are girls," they say. Or, "At the birth of a son all are glad, but about a daughter people mourn." "When a boy comes into the world, there is peace; when it is a girl, there comes nothing."[2]

Whatever Jairus so far may have thought about women, seeing the predicament of his one and only daughter breaks his heart. Maybe Jairus doesn't realize how void and hypocritical religion in Israel has become. The prayers of Jewish men who daily praise God self-righteously that they were not born women are abominable to Him. Talking about the Law has become a mockery, since one of God's most central orders of Creation is being trampled upon. Every Jew knows from the first lines of the Holy Scriptures that God created male and female equally after His own image, that He also equally entrusted them with the care for the earth and its inhabitants. Man and woman are called to be equal partners—to love, complement, and serve one another. The Jews have deviated drastically from this primal goal.

The esteem for women by most religious leaders in Jairus' time is far below God's standard. Jairus was never so painfully aware of this as now. Jesus is different, he knows. But Jesus is also a Jew and a man. How will He react? Will He let His important work be interrupted for a woman, a child at that? This child is everything to Jairus, but what value has she in the eyes of the Lord?

Jairus need not have worried. Jesus gets up immediately and goes with him. But the walk to his house does not develop as smoothly as Jairus hoped it would. The pressing crowd prohibits them from moving quickly. Then there is the torment of an unexpected delay. A sick woman seeks help from Jesus, just as he has. (Remarkable. She has been sick for the same number of years as Jairus' daughter is old: twelve.)

Just because Jesus decides to come with Jairus right away doesn't mean that this woman is of less interest to Him. To the people, she is of much lower rank than the leader of the synagogue. But from Jesus she gets full opportunity to relate the misery of those past twelve years. Jairus has to learn that Jesus takes every woman—including this sick one who is an outcast in society—seriously.

What Jairus was afraid of, what he by all means wanted to prevent, happens. During the delay his child dies.

"Don't bother the teacher any more," is the message from home. The implied meaning is clear. "This Man obviously can heal the sick, but over death He holds no control." Apparently forgotten is the fact that Jesus very recently raised someone from the dead: the son of a widow in Nain.

Jesus ignores these words. "Don't be afraid," He says to Jairus. "Just believe, and she will be healed." The words are to the father a life buoy to which he clings.

These words may be reassuring, but arriving at Jairus' house, the reality is different. Although the girl has died a very brief time ago, the mourning women and flute players have already arrived. From the house of the deceased a deafening noise receives Jesus and Jairus. Professional mourners who are paid for their lamentations have already taken possession of the house. Naturally there is sincere sympathy with the bereaved parents and intense sorrow about the death of their only daughter. Add to this the fact that a prominent citizen is involved. This possibly makes the mourning even louder.

Jesus watches the tumult and says to the mourners, "Stop wailing. She is not dead but asleep."

(Bible commentators differ in opinion here. There are those who think of the sleep of death, as with Lazarus. Others believe that the girl, who appeared to be dead, was asleep in a coma. Even then Jesus most likely saved her life. Climatic conditions in Palestine necessitated burial within a matter of hours. Consequently, people were sometimes buried alive, as some excavations of tombs have proven.)

Then the shallowness of the mourning is revealed. The mourners are not really happy to hear these hopeful words that apparently not all is lost. They laugh at Jesus. It is one of the many moments when the Son of God suffers here on earth.

Jesus' suffering is not restricted to the Cross, although there it is at its peak. Every day of His life on earth He suffers physically, for He is familiar with sickness and fatigue. But His deepest pain is spiritual. Jesus, who is sensitive by nature, suffers from the people: their lack of love, their pedantry, and their superficiality. He suffers from the contempt and rejection of sinful men. Jesus, being without sin Himself, observes the horror of sin in the often insensitive behavior in human relationships. The Lord knows sin, not by personal experience but because He sees it operating in the lives around Him. In this way He suffers here.

Jesus sends practically everyone away. Only Peter, James, John, and the father and mother enter the room with Him where the girl is. As parents, dad and mom stand together. To Western ears this is natural. But among the Jews of Jesus' time it is different. Here the father sees to the affairs of his unwed daughter. (He arranges her engagement and, by himself or with other men, her wedding. The mother has nothing to say in the matter.)

Jesus places the woman side by side with the man, the mother next to the father. He shows understanding for this mother's sorrow. She certainly doesn't suffer any less. He takes her no less seriously than her husband.

Jesus then speaks only two words: *"Talitha koum!'* (which means, 'Little girl, I say to you, get up!')." To the girl they make the difference between life and death. With the pressure of His hand upon hers, the girl gets up immediately. She lives! She is completely healed, for she gets up and walks around.

Jesus' practical advice is to give her something to eat. In their bewilderment the parents have overlooked the need for food. For many days during the illness the child has not taken a solid meal. What is needed now is not a miracle. The laws of nature just need to take their course.

Just a day in the life of Jesus. But it is *the* day of their lives for the three women who meet Him. The sick woman receives complete health and exchanges a life without purpose for a new acceptance in society. The young girl who was dead starts her life afresh and with a new perspective. Jairus' wife receives what she didn't ask for, something she probably had not even missed: an awareness of her self-worth. To Jesus she is not just the wife of her husband and the mother of her child. She is of great value in and of herself. She is one of the "daughters" about whom Isaiah speaks: precious, honored, and loved by God.[3]

Humanity didn't find it easy to understand God's plan about the role of woman next to man. In Christendom, as in society, an unseen measuring stick is often applied that rates the male higher than the female. God endowed woman with certain unique characteristics necessary to a complete society. But because men have made it difficult for women to exercise those characteristics, all relationships have suffered irreparable damage.

Christian women are also guilty themselves. Whether consciously or not, they often underrate themselves. They don't apply the standard mentioned by Isaiah that God desires of His daughters. Neglecting this high calling, women indirectly underestimate the high price Christ paid for them with His life. Underestimating yourself is often as sinful as overestimating yourself. In both cases God is robbed of His honor.

I remember a flourishing Bible study group in which women were actively engaged—until, due to reorganization, men were added to the group. Soon only the male members participated—not because they wanted to dominate, but because the women, unaware of it, removed themselves to the background.

In talks with couples, I sometimes catch myself being inclined to rate the husband's input higher than the wife's contribution.

When the first grandchild of Queen Juliana of the Netherlands, Prince Willem-Alexander, was born, a woman shouted enthusiastically, "A boy! A crown prince!" Later it was known that grandmother Juliana was hurt by this. "Would a crown princess have been of less value?" she asked. It was a good question in a country that for several generations now is greatly indebted to its excellent queens.

Among the events of that day in Galilee, what happens to Jairus' wife seems to be least striking to us. Yet this may have the most far-reaching meaning in the long run because it points prophetically to the purpose of Jesus' coming to earth. He came to break down high barriers—not only between God and men, but also between various groups of the human race itself, divided as it is by race, sex, wealth, and so on. Jesus' attitude toward the wife of Jairus is more than an individual case of comfort in sorrow. It also throws His light on godly principles in the relationship between male and female.

At His death Jesus breaks all the measuring sticks that people use. From these He makes the cross on which He Himself is tortured. He dies so that double standards will be abolished forever.

"He died for all, so that those who live should no longer live for themselves, but only for him who died and was raised to life for their sake. No longer, then, do we judge anyone by human standards."[4]

God expects us to look at the world this way. Moreover, He expects us to apply this perspective in our lives.

NOTES: 1. Read Matthew 9:18-25, Mark 5:21-43, and Luke 8:40-56.
      2. Peter Ketter, *Christ and Women*, page 70
      3. Isaiah 43:4-7
      4. 2 Corinthians 5:15-16 (TEV)

QUESTIONS FOR PERSONAL OR GROUP STUDY

1. Jesus engaged the following people in the exciting event of raising someone from the dead:
   - Jairus
   - Jairus' wife

- Jairus' daughter
- the disciples
- the mourners.

In our modern era, reporters from the press, radio, and television might be right there to cover such an exceptional occurrence. Try to imagine that you are a reporter. What questions would you ask? What answers would you expect? Tip: Journalists usually work with the questions *who* (who was it all about), *what* (what happened), *where* (where it happened), *how* (how things developed), and *why.*

2. What impressed you most of all in this story?

9
He Gives a Woman His Undivided Attention

"A woman was there who had been subject to bleed-
ing for twelve years, but no one could heal her. She
came up behind him and touched the edge of his
cloak, and immediately her bleeding stopped."
(Luke 8:43-44)[1]

Hopeless. Trapped. Completely frustrated. That's the way she feels. For twelve years she has been consulting doctors, spending her last dime on them. Unfortunately, without any solution. Her troubles have only increased. Medically she is a hopeless case.

One hundred and forty-four months. More than four thousand days and nights she has experienced blood flowing from her body. She has felt increasingly weaker and more tired, growing less and less secure through the years.

From a Jewish point of view this is a most humbling illness, but in Jesus' days it is very common. Besides regular medication, it is treated by means based on sheer superstition, such as carrying the ashes of an ostrich egg on the patient's body.

How many well-meaning suggestions she has considered over the years cannot be counted anymore. Over and again there has been a spark of hope, but always followed by disappointment.

The illness has taken from this woman all her physical strength. It has gradually devoured all her financial resources and brought her to the bottom of her emotional resources as well. Ill, poor, and lonely—that is the situation in which she finds herself. The time of health insurance and benefits for the ailing, of all kinds of medical and social provisions, has not yet arrived. The result is total isolation.

Her problems don't stop with physical, emotional, and financial concerns. They also threaten her spiritual life. Jewish leaders see a causal relationship between illness and sin. Is somebody ill? Then in their eyes he is a sinner. Jesus' disciples don't see this any differently. When they meet a blind man they ask, "Who sinned, this man or his parents?"[2]

This woman's illness has an extra troublesome side. The Jewish Law declares such a patient unclean, condemned to live in seclusion.[3] Thus for this woman there is no room in the women's section of the synagogue. On the Sabbath she cannot listen with others to the reading of the Law. When other women on Jewish festive days travel with their relatives to Jerusalem, she remains at home. How lonely her existence has become.

For some Jewish women in our time, little has changed. Jewish women in Ethiopia in 1985, during their monthly "uncleanness," are relegated to live separately in little hovels at the edge of their village. Their territory is marked by stones that they are not allowed to pass over. Men cannot approach this female territory.[4]

Social life for this first-century Jewish woman is also impossible. She cannot just drop in on her neighbors or relatives since all she touches turns "unclean." She misses the daily outing to the local well with other females, where they exchange the latest village gossip. She is hardly better off than a leper, who is literally expelled from the community. As far as loneliness is concerned, her situation is little brighter.

Does she have a husband? Then she must stay away from him, too. There is no possibility of a normal wedded life. If she is without a man, then her outlook on marriage is extremely dim. The male influence in her life, which every woman needs, is next to absent.

Add to her misery the difficulty in caring for daily body hygiene. She must do without bathing facilities, deodorants, and other products that are so helpful to modern women. No doubt her misery is complete.

But one day this woman hears something about a man named Jesus. It seems that He is a messenger of God to His people. Jesus brings to remembrance the earlier times of the prophets and the miracles they performed. Certainly one of the most remarkable women of her people, Miriam,[5] and later the Syrian officer Naaman,[6] had both been healed from incurable diseases. Now miracles like that are being done by Jesus of Nazareth. The recent healing of a man possessed by many demons at the other side of the lake in the land of the Gerasenes, and the two thousand pigs that were drowned afterwards, is the talk of the day throughout the entire area.

Her illness took much away from her, but it did not take away her faith. In spite of twelve years of trouble and sorrow her faith has not been totally shipwrecked. So she gains confidence that Jesus can and will release her from her problem. But there are questions.

First a practical question. Does she have the strength to reach Jesus where He is? Will her weak body keep up in a crowd? Will bystanders recognize her and block the way? Will the Jewish leaders, such sticklers of the Law, let her go through? And will Jesus' disciples conclude that she is a nuisance who is holding things up? She, the unclean one, doesn't have the right to mix with the healthy. She is a danger to them.

There is a still deeper question. Not only is she ill, but she is a woman. Conscientious rabbis forbid their fellow rabbis to greet a woman in public. A rabbi is not even allowed to speak with his own wife, daughter, or sister in public. There are Pharisees who do not even want to *see* a woman in the street. They are referred to as the bruised and bleeding Pharisees. When these men encounter a woman in the street, they shut their eyes, blindly walking into walls or houses. A rabbi who is observed holding a conversation with a woman in the street jeopardizes his good name! If this Jesus is like them, she doesn't stand a chance. Will Jesus react like those spiritual leaders of her people, or is He different? Jesus has healed many men. Does He also care about women? Indeed, He healed Peter's mother-in-law, but that was after the intercession of His disciples.

Nobody takes the initiative for this afflicted woman. There are no friends to bring her to Jesus. She must go all by herself, alone.

The problems are great but not insurmountable. Long illness easily leads to discouragement and apathy, but it can also result in faith, courage, and deep reflection. This is what happens to this woman. Suffering stimulates her faith and courage. Perhaps she feels intuitively that Jesus' approach to women goes back to the original meaning of Creation, where God created male and female in complete equality. God intended a future where there would be no difference between male and female.[7]

Necessity is the mother of invention. In spite of her faith and her courage, the woman takes a modest approach. She doesn't expect Jesus to visit her house, nor does she look for a special word. Rather, she stays anonymous. The fact that she is too shy to frankly admit her embarrassing problem naturally plays a role. So the thought arises to touch Jesus from behind. She will recognize Him, a rabbi, even from the back by the white tassels of His robe.

Slowly she shuffles forward. All around her are pushing people. Next to Jesus walks Jairus, one of the heads of the synagogue. He is the last person she wants to meet just now! Jairus represents the Law; he can throw her plans completely. It takes courage now to go on.

Coming closer to Jesus, she is drawn toward Him like a magnet. She can do it. She will not go back. She puts her hand forward and touches Him. At the same moment a power she has never known shocks through her body. It is as though her heart stops pounding. The miracle has happened! Her bleeding has stopped! Having suffered the agony of this infirmity for many years, she has learned to listen to her body. There is no doubt: she is healed!

Just then Jesus turns around, His eyes searchingly moving over the crowd. He asks, "Who touched me?"

The disciples find it a somewhat foolish question. Peter, always ready with an answer, says what the others are thinking. "Master, the people are crowding and pressing against you." He implies that Jesus' question is somewhat absurd, since many people in the crowd are touching Him.

Jesus responds, "Someone touched me; I know that power has gone out from me."

The woman is now forced to overcome her shyness. Nervous, trembling all over, she steps forward. The joy of healing turns into fear. The healing that she appropriated slyly—will the Lord take this away from her? Will she be disappointed again? According to the Law, Jesus, because He has been touched by this woman, has now also become unclean. Will she be punished for that?

Now she stands eye-to-eye with the Savior. In His look she doesn't read disapproval because of her uncleanness, but understanding and love. She senses no rejection because she is a woman, but only acceptance.

Now it proves that Jesus differs completely from the other religious leaders of His time. The bystanders are astonished that this rabbi treats a woman just as He would a man.

That is new. She receives no less attention than does the esteemed Jairus, who impatiently fears that this delay may prove disastrous for his deathly ill daughter. His consent, however, is not even asked for.

The woman feels as though she is being scrutinized to the very roots of her existence. Her entire life lies open to the searching look of this kind rabbi. She forgets everything and everyone standing around her. The crowds—she doesn't see them. Jairus—even he doesn't bother her. The only one she sees is Jesus—Jesus alone. All she can do is humbly and reverently bow before Him. He accepts her tribute, for it rightfully belongs to Him. He is the Son of God, God Himself.

Then the doors of long pent-up feelings open up. She tells Him the entire truth: all the misery she has experienced, the rejection of her people, and her own self-repugnance. Her deep loneliness, discouragement, sorrow, and rage—she spills it all out. She has never met a person who listens to her so intently.

She, a woman, openly recounts her intimate concerns amid many curious eyes and ears—to a man in the street. Here is someone, finally, who understands how deeply she has suffered.

The Great Physician lets her talk. Verbalizing old grief and acknowledging personal failing cleanses her mind and spirit just as her body is cleansed. Eye-to-eye with the Savior of the world, she becomes a new creature in every way.

"Take heart," He says—words that have been said a hundred times, but never, as now, by someone who can give actual power to them.

"Your faith has healed you." It has made her whole. This is precisely what happens. A broken life becomes whole in body, mind, and spirit.

"Go in peace and be freed from your suffering." With the

promise that this woman's healing is total and permanent, Jesus restores her in all her relationships: her relationship with God and all her other interpersonal connections. All women, but in particular those who have experienced deep loneliness, need this kind of affirmation.

Jesus frees this woman of a stained past and gives her a new future. This open declaration of her healing has put her right back into society. To the people of her town, Jesus says, You shall no longer avoid her. To the leader of the synagogue, He says, You must cordially welcome her in the services again. Because the Son of God makes her free, she is free indeed.[8]

The woman who was willing to be satisfied with a quiet healing receives much more than she expected. We do not know what became of her, what the practical outcome of her liberation was, whether she mingled with the women who accompanied Jesus and His disciples or stayed in her hometown.

Just as she stepped forward out of anonymity, she steps back, oblivious to the fact that she would be the only woman mentioned in Scripture who personally took the initiative for her own healing by the Great Physician.

There are no doubt many women in Israel who are ill. We read of only a few who are cured, usually because of the intercession of others who approach Jesus. Women dare less often to make an appeal to Him. They allow themselves to be trapped by prevailing public opinion and age-old tradition. But this woman understands that the Lord has come to set aside unfair role patterns and rusty taboos, that He judges people according to faith and not by sex. By this she is a timeless example to all women everywhere.

In our day we call such a woman assertive, someone with a healthy conviction of her self-worth, and draw certain positive conclusions from that. She is seen as an example of what

faith, courage, and a proper form of self-esteem can bring
about. Her story proves that Jesus honors such an attitude,
provided that it is based on faith.

Do the men among the bystanders, Jairus and the disciples, understand the extent of what takes place? Do they see
that more than a healing has happened? Jesus here illustrates
how men and women should treat one another. The good
news that should be preached all over the world is a message
that liberates all people—including women. Possibilities of
personal realization and development are for all, both men
and women, provided that they have personal encounters
with Jesus Christ.

An objective assessment of the past two thousand years
of human history discloses that we still have a long way to go.
Men and women are too often seen through different glasses.
A member of the Dutch parliament experienced this as she
returned with several male colleagues from the French capital
after attending a conference on unilateral disarmament.

"Where did you come from?" asked the customs officer.

"Paris," she replied.

"And, little lady, was it nice shopping?" asked the man.

It is good for men and women alike that this Bible story
has been recorded. Right on the very first pages of the Bible
God says that He created male and female with a true sense of
equality and a mutual assignment. Tradition has covered this
original plan over with a thick layer of dust. Jesus breaks
through our counterfeit order of the sexes and again places
the original godly plan in full light with convincing deeds.

NOTES: 1. Read Matthew 9:20-22, Mark 5:25-34, and Luke 8:43-48.
        2. John 9:2
        3. Leviticus 15:19-30
        4. *Trouw* (newspaper from the Netherlands), 1/26/85, page 23
        5. Numbers 12:10-15

6. 2 Kings 5:1-15
7. Galatians 3:28
8. John 8:36

QUESTIONS FOR PERSONAL OR GROUP STUDY

1. What is the relationship in the Old Testament between disease and obedience toward God? (Deuteronomy 28:1-2, 15,21-22).

2. What does Jesus say about the purpose of sickness and suffering in John 9:1-3 and 11:4? Can you give examples where this was achieved during Jesus' ministry?

3. List the inhibitions this woman had to overcome to mix among the people and touch Jesus.

4. This woman "told [Jesus] the whole truth" (Mark 5:33). What do you think she said and experienced in her encounter with Jesus?

5. According to Jesus, what caused this woman's healing? Can you name other examples of this phenomenon?

6. What can we, men and women alike, still learn from this story?

10
He Doesn't Use Two Measuring Sticks

"The teachers of the law and the Pharisees brought in a woman caught in adultery. They made her stand before the group and said to Jesus, 'Teacher, this woman was caught in the act of adultery. In the Law Moses commanded us to stone such women. Now what do you say?'"

(John 8:3-5)[1]

The Feast of Tabernacles, one of the three great Jewish feasts, is just over. Every mature and healthy Jew who lives within the range of sixteen miles of the holy city of Jerusalem is obliged to attend. The annual harvest festival lasts a week, and the entire family takes part in it.

At the feast Jesus makes wonderful promises. Those who believe in Him will receive the Holy Spirit and great joy will be the result. Being filled with joy themselves, they bring joy to others. Their hearts will be a fountain from which streams of fresh and living water will flow continually.[2]

Many become convinced that Jesus is the promised Messiah. Other are critical and doubtful. Both groups are now present at the Temple courtyard, interested in what He has to say. The religious leaders also remain critical and reject Jesus. Thirst for God and a desire for the Holy Spirit is foreign to most of them. On the contrary, they are driven by a growing aversion and bitterness against Jesus. They harbor only one thought: Jesus must be done away with. His voice must definitely be silenced.

Under these circumstances a woman who is caught in

adultery is brought in. She is unaware that the religious
leaders are using her as bait to catch Jesus. The hard, closed
faces of the men who drag her to the Temple area don't
promise much good. I am up against real opposition, she
thinks. Agreed, she has been caught in adultery, but why
make a major case out of that?

But the law on adultery is technically inflexible, although
it is rarely enforced—just another example of pharisaical
hypocrisy. The teachers of the Law and the Pharisees proudly
push the woman through the crowd until she stands before
Jesus.

"Teacher, this woman was caught in the act of adultery.
In the Law Moses commanded us to stone such women. Now
what do you say?"

Cold and heartless are their words. Sure, they are right.
According to the Law the woman must die. The Law registers
offense and indicates the need for punishment. It offers no
pardon. These men are not, however, motivated primarily by
respect for the Law. The sin of the woman is not their first
concern. She is only a pawn on the chessboard to stalemate
Jesus.

The hypocrisy of these religious leaders is obvious. They
refer to a law they otherwise hardly consider. The life of this
woman is of so little value to them that they coldbloodedly
plan her death, only to give rein to their hatred against Jesus.

It is a sly plan. How can Jesus possibly escape them? They
plan to catch Him in His own words. If He says yes, do stone
her, He collides with the Roman law, which denies Jews the
right to execute the death sentence. As a friend of the people
on the fringes of society, He also loses His good name. But if
He says no, pardon her, He then refuses the Law of Moses.
Jesus, who accuses the Jews of neglecting the Law, cannot
omit Himself what He expects others to do.

Miserable leaders they are. They treat people as mere

"things" to be manipulated. Even Jesus doesn't escape them. As scholars of the Law who are consulted in matters of controversy, they have authority, but they certainly don't use it with understanding and sympathy. True authority is interested in why the offender did wrong and how he can be helped to repent and reform. We see nothing of the kind here. Rather, these men behave like moral watchdogs, trying to tear the sinner to pieces, instead of shepherds of the flock. The feelings of the woman are of no concern to them.

When the well-known English preacher George Whitefield saw a criminal on the way to the gallows, he said, "There, but for the grace of God, go I." This kind of empathy with the plight of others is foreign to these Jewish leaders.

The fact that the accused is a woman makes the neglect of her human dignity no doubt even more acceptable. Such blanket disrespect is a problem that after two thousand years is still not remedied, unfortunately. Paul Tournier says that men often still fail to see a woman as a person. He writes about woman, "The fact is that she has been treated as a thing even more than men have. Men . . . are more ready to manipulate women, both physically and morally, than to seek a person-to-person relationship with them."[3]

Jesus is different. He cannot be accused of not understanding those who are oppressed or dealt with unfairly. He doesn't agree with those who give women a secondary rating. The quick judgment the accusers hope for is not forthcoming.

Jesus keeps silent . . . stoops down . . . looks at the ground and writes.

Some think that Jesus hides His face out of a sense of shame. The disrespectful way these men offend the woman hurts Jesus. Jesus suffers to see the lack of understanding and sympathy of those who are in a position of responsibility. It hurts when religious leaders don't follow His example and show respect toward women.

Both hatred for Jesus and neglect of a human being bring these men to a double standard and a one-sided interpretation of the Law. The Law of Moses requires that the man and woman guilty of adultery be stoned together outside the city gate. Rightly so; *both* are guilty.

The interpretation of the Law here applied with this woman is hypocritical and hard. It is also shortsighted. This woman can do many things independently. Without any help at all she is capable of lying, stealing, even murder. She, however, cannot play solo adultery. As with a game of tennis or chess, two are needed in sexual intercourse. That leaders of a nation in their folly overlook this obvious fact is remarkable, to put it mildly.

It is directly after this incident that Jesus says of Himself, "I am the light of the world." This light exposes the self-righteous attitude of the Pharisees and teachers of religion.

It also exposes the life of the woman. Jesus knows what or who induced her to adultery. He knows whether loneliness or neglect brought her to such a situation. Has she possibly fled from marriage with a man she doesn't love? In many countries this is still the case. In the East a girl is still an object of exchange. Her father, uncle, or brothers negotiate with the matrimonial agent. Consent of the bride is only a minor formality. King Saul twice gave a daughter in marriage without consulting her.[4]

There are all kinds of suppositions about why Jesus remains silent. Possibly He wants to gain time. Or is He counseling together with His Father? Just a short time later He says, "I pass judgment on no one. But if I do judge, my decisions are right, because I am not alone. I stand with the Father who sent me."[5] In any event, the accusers receive an opportunity to reconsider—which they don't do.

There are also various thoughts about what Jesus is writing down. Interesting is the Armenian translation: "He

Himself, bowing His head, was writing with His finger on the earth to declare their sins; and they were seeing their several sins on the stones."[6]

Finally, He straightens up to speak. "If any one of you is without sin, let him be the first to throw a stone at her." Stones are everywhere in Israel. The woman fears that her last hour has come. Sharp, pointed stones will cause bleeding. Heavy stones will break and bruise her.

But all of a sudden it becomes obvious that the religious leaders have used measuring sticks to which they cannot measure up themselves. They apply laws they don't keep themselves. Not one of them can be held blameless. Even the eldest among them has no clear conscience. He leaves first. After him the others shirk away, embarrassed. If the truth Jesus knows about them were exposed, they would be judged and there would be other deaths. Somebody titled this story, quite understandably, "Jesus and the Adulterous Men."

Jesus, meanwhile, starts writing on the ground again. When He looks up, only He and the woman remain.

"Where are they? Has no one condemned you?" It is the first time He talks to her personally.

"No one, sir."

"Then neither do I condemn you. Go now and leave your life of sin."

The only person who has a right to judge her—for He is without sin—sets her free. At the same time He puts her on the right track. Whoever draws the conclusion that Jesus apparently takes sin lightly is mistaken. His warning to stop sinning proves that. He doesn't call her adultery permissible weakness or adjusting to free morals. He plainly calls it *sin*.

In all His teachings Jesus holds high the purity and indissoluble nature of marriage. Immorality He never condones. He deals with other women guilty of adultery (the Samaritan woman and the woman in the house of Simon the

Pharisee). In all of these cases, Jesus' attitude is neither denigrating nor condescending. He makes a clear distinction between sin, which has to be condemned, and the sinner, to whom He reaches out with understanding.

Remarkable also is that Jesus pronounces no special judgment over sexual misbehavior. He disapproves of all sins. But the law of love operates within Him to motivate people toward repentance and faith.

"Go now and leave your life of sin." A more concise yet complete summary of forgiveness and reform is hardly possible. It addresses the unrighteous and unacceptable nature of sin, but it opens at the same time the prospect of forgiveness and a new future. It is Jesus' warning not to return to the old way of life. This encounter makes it clear how Jesus does away with a double standard, how He objects to the different treatment given men and women.

Not long after this event, a cross is erected at Calvary. There Jesus dies in order to reconcile the relationship between God and men, as well as between men and men, and between men and women. But what has the world, and especially the Church, learned since then?

A number of years ago in Israel, not far from where this story occurred, a couple appear before a rabbinical court in Tel Aviv in connection with the dissolution of their marriage. This happens on the request of the wife after her spouse has long and openly been unfaithful to her.

In her book *Or Did I Dream a Dream?*,[7] Ruth Dayan, the ex-wife of the late Israeli General Moshe Dayan, tells of the humiliation of that ceremony to her as a woman. She, the innocent party, was "repudiated" and had to make all kinds of promises to protect her unfaithful husband. He, the guilty one, needed to make no promises toward her. Until just recently men have been judged far less critically for sexual misbehavior than women.

And not only in Israel. Recently a young man, talking about faithfulness in marriage, said on the Dutch television, "I would appreciate for my wife to be monogamous. For myself, I stick to a wider notion in this respect."

This measuring with a double standard is also an infringement of human rights. While discriminating against a woman, man discriminates against himself.

What impression does this story have on Christians, those of us who are calling ourselves followers of Jesus Christ? How do we respond to it? This question has no unanimous answer. But as responsible men and women of God, we must grapple with this question—with Jesus' perspective in mind.

NOTES: 1. Read John 8:2-11. (Some manuscripts do not include John 7:53-8:11. Therefore, some Bible translations put it in brackets or in a footnote.)
2. John 7:37-39
3. Paul Tournier, *The Gift of Feeling*, pages 12,28
4. 1 Samuel 18:17,27
5. John 8:15-16
6. William Barclay, *The Daily Study Bible*, "The Gospel of John," Volume 2 (Edinburgh, Scotland: The Saint Andrew Press, 1983), page 3
7. Ruth Dayan and Helga Dudman, *Or Did I Dream a Dream?* (London: Weidenfeld and Nicolson, 1973)

QUESTIONS FOR PERSONAL OR GROUP STUDY

1. How did Jesus speak about the Pharisees and why? (Matthew 23:13-15, 23-33).

2. What precisely did the Jewish law on adultery state? Who was named first, the man or the woman? (Leviticus 20:10, Deuteronomy 22:22-24).

3. In what way were two measuring sticks used in this case? How should the laws of God be applied?

4. What does the Bible say about the purity and indissoluble nature of marriage? (Exodus 20:14, 1 Corinthians 6:13,16, Hebrews 13:4).

5. What struck you most in this story?

6. In what way do men and women measure with double standards in our time? On what do you base your own perspective? What can be done to reconcile such double standards more closely to Jesus' example?

11
He Recognizes a Woman's Worth

"Then should not this woman, a daughter of Abraham, whom Satan has kept bound for eighteen long years, be set free on the Sabbath day from what bound her?"

(Luke 13:16)[1]

It is Sabbath, somewhere in a synagogue in Israel. It is the last time we will meet Jesus there. This is His final trip to Jerusalem. Every step now brings His crucifixion a step closer. In spite of this coming agony, Jesus doesn't close His eyes to the needs of the people around Him.

Suddenly, in the middle of His teaching, Jesus stops. His eyes detect a severely crippled woman who sits in the back section reserved for women. A curvature of the spine has bent her in such a way that she has not been able to stand erect for a long time. The faces of the people around her are no longer familiar to her. They, in turn, know the lines of her neck and shoulders better than her features. Her suffering started eighteen years ago and has only increased since then.

To everybody's amazement, the Lord addresses this invalid personally. "Woman, you are set free from your infirmity."

Whether Jesus goes to where she sits or calls her to come to Him is not recorded, nor is it all that important. But at the moment He places His hands on her back it straightens. She can stand upright again!

What she sees first are not the faces of the people, the tree tops, or the blue sky—things she couldn't see properly for a long time. Her first gaze is straight into the face of Jesus. There she reads love, compassion, and empathy. She also perceives the holiness and glory of God. Her reaction is the only right one. She thanks God and honors Him for what He has done for her!

The past sickness covers a large portion of her life. They were years filled with pain and tension concerning an insecure future. Like any Jew, she also wrestled with the question about the relationship between sickness and sin. But suffering hasn't embittered her, nor has it separated her from God. In spite of much painful trouble she has come this Saturday morning to the synagogue. There is no reason for us to believe that she knew Jesus would be there nor that she came specifically for healing. She receives it as a present she did not expect.

The miracle happens in a meeting of believing Jews that is arranged to honor God. One could expect that those present would share her joy and spontaneously praise God with her. But there are reasons for the cold reception.

For nearly three years Jesus has traveled the country. He has healed many sick people and even resurrected some from the dead. He has multiplied scanty provisions of food to feed thousands. And this itinerant rabbi always seems ready to have theological discussions with religious leaders or to listen to mothers of small children. Everyone who seeks Him receives His undivided attention. Nobody is ever sent away. One would think that Jesus, as a result, could expect good will, at least from the leaders of the people. They can certainly judge Him on the basis of His extraordinary merits.

But their first thought proves to be to rap Him on the knuckles. Their spokesman here is the leader of this synagogue. He boldly objects to this healing. Haughtily he dares to reprimand Jesus, although he lacks the courage to do it directly.

"There are six days for work. So come and be healed on those days, not on the Sabbath," he sneers indignantly to no one in particular. These are heartless words, words that disregard the woman's human dignity. They stab at her self-respect.

He talks about her impersonally, as though she doesn't matter. Would this man react in the same way if, for instance, a Pharisee with whom he is on friendly terms were healed instead of a common woman? The leader of the synagogue overlooks further the fact that the initiative for healing started with Jesus, not with the woman. This man suffers from blindness because he doesn't want to see.

As the synagogue ruler, he, above anyone else, should be grateful that this miracle happened in his synagogue. But he feels no joy that the pain and the handicap of this woman belong to the past. He is not happy that a new future has unexpectedly opened up for her. Nor is he impressed by the power of the Lord. Jesus' love for the helpless in society leaves him cold. He reacts with rigid formalism and legalism. According to him, healing equals work, which the Law forbids on the Sabbath day. He in fact accuses Jesus of considering a human being more important than the Sabbath. This shows his distorted interpretation of the Law.

The Jews use the term "law" in four different ways: first, for the Ten Commandments; second, for the five books of Moses; third, for the entire Old Testament; fourth, for the oral law, or the law of the scribes. At the time of Jesus, this oral law (later called the Mishnah) is usually what is meant.

The Ten Commandments and the Old Testament, with only a few exceptions, mention simply the broad principles every human should use to order his or her personal life. The scribes added to this an enormous number of detailed rules and regulations that they considered the law for both themselves and others. (The Mishnah fills a book of some eight hundred pages. Commentaries on these—the Talmud—consist of twelve printed Jerusalem volumes and sixty Babylonian!)

In the days of Jesus, strict orthodox Jews consider it a service to God to keep thousands of very technical legal rules and regulations. To them life, death, and eternal destiny all depend on this legal accomplishment.

The oral law considers healing on the Sabbath as work that is allowed only in cases of life-threatening danger or sudden deterioration of the patient. Thus a Jew is allowed to dress a wound with a simple piece of cotton wool, but no ointment is to be administered.

Jesus objects strongly to this contrived interpretation. He lives according to the true meaning of the Law, that is, to honor God and to respect fellow humans and yourself.[2] His interpretation is aimed at life, not at harsh technicalities devised to catch people in their snares. Earlier, when the Pharisees "caught" Jesus in the same "offense," He answered that it is lawful to do good on the Sabbath.[3] He has summarized this idea in the Golden Rule: "In everything, do to others what you would have them do to you."[4]

Jesus has only one word for what is happening here: hypocrisy! "You hypocrites! Doesn't each of you on the Sabbath untie his ox or donkey from the stall and lead it out to give it water? Then should not this woman, a daughter of Abraham, whom Satan has kept bound for eighteen long years, be set free on the Sabbath day from what bound her?"

Indeed, with the permission of the rabbis, animals could be released from their stalls on the Sabbath in order to drink. In this land of Israel, where water is scarce, long distances sometimes have to be traveled for animals to receive a drink. If that cannot be called work. . . .

Jesus puts His rebuke in the form of a question. The

leader of the synagogue needs to see for himself how selective his indignation really is. He needs to be unmasked—to recognize that he is using two entirely different measuring sticks, that he applies the Law differently to himself than to others, that a thirsty animal in its stable is more important to him than this woman.

But the people must wonder whether they are hearing correctly. Does Jesus call this woman a daughter of Abraham? That is unheard of! Never before has this been said of a *woman!*

As descendants of their patriarch Abraham, Jewish men proudly call themselves sons of Abraham. But never has there been mention of a daughter of Abraham—until Jesus does it. That is because men and women receive from Him the same degree of honor and respect.

Abraham is not only the forefather of the Jews, but he is also the spiritual father of all believers. Abraham is a man known to be the friend of God.

Does Jesus refer to a relationship between the woman's sickness and her faith? This is not a foreign thought to the Jews. Jesus also mentions in the same breath that the woman is "a daughter of Abraham" and "bound by Satan." This, too, does not sound strange to Jewish ears. They know the Old Testament story about Job. Job, an exceptional, God-fearing man, suffered terribly and incomprehensibly due to the attacks of Satan. Is this situation perhaps similar?

This woman also experiences God's special attention and blessing, just as Job did. By way of her healing, God's name is widely honored. From the men of the land, this woman receives less attention than the beasts in their stables, and yet Jesus mentions her in one breath with Abraham!

To the leaders of the synagogue and others present she becomes a sign. When from now on they see her walking straight and healthy, she will be a reminder that Jesus is opposed to hypocritical conduct. That He hates and exposes unequal treatment. That He, very much against the code of His time, doesn't discriminate against women.

After eighteen years of sickness and pain, to be able to move about freely is a precious gift. The tourist health-cure industry is increasingly spreading from the West to Eastern Europe. Even in our day, people take much trouble to be cured physically and to alleviate chronic diseases.

Regaining her self-respect and feeling of self-worth is to this woman no less precious than recovering her health. During times of long illness, without hope of improvement, it is often difficult not to lose heart or become spiritually unbalanced. Pain may directly attack the body, but it also attacks the mind. This is especially true for Jews who consider sickness a judgment from God.

I remember two women who were simultaneously experiencing low ebbs in their lives. One, an author, had serious physical problems that made her practically a captive in her own home. In her work, however, she was productive and appreciated. The other, a scientist, was perfectly healthy, could move about as she desired, but felt curtailed in her career. Being a woman, she was passed over at promotion time. She felt that she would miss out on a great future.

Both of these women had difficult times. But it was my impression that, apart from the differences in personality structure, the first one experienced the limiting situation as less painful because her feeling of self-worth was not injured.

Jesus understands this. Therefore He cures this crippled woman not only physically but spiritually as well. By calling her a daughter of Abraham, He recognizes her worth as a person, as a believer. This she needs more than anything else

---

NOTES: 1. Read Luke 13:10-17.
       2. Matthew 22:37-40

3. Matthew 12:9-14
4. Matthew 7:12

QUESTIONS FOR PERSONAL OR GROUP STUDY

1. How highly does God estimate the worth of an individual? (Psalm 8:4-8, 139:13-16, John 3:16).

2. What kind of essential distinction does He make between male and female? (Genesis 1:26-28, Romans 2:11, Galatians 3:28).

3. What does God think about using different standards of measurement? (Deuteronomy 25:13-16, Proverbs 20:10).

4. What made Abraham so exceptional? (Genesis 12:1-3, Romans 4:18-21, Hebrews 11:8-12).

5. How should a son or a daughter of Abraham be recognized? (Luke 3:8, 19:8-9). In what way does this woman show that she possesses this characteristic?

6. How do you identify personally with the situation of this woman?

12
He Appreciates a Woman's Wit

"A Canaanite woman from that vicinity came to him, crying out, 'Lord, Son of David, have mercy on me! My daughter is suffering terribly from demon-possession.' Jesus did not answer a word. . . ."
(Matthew 15:22-23)[1]

Does Jesus again seek rest? Once before when He wanted to withdraw with His disciples, rest turned out to be out of the question. People figured out where He was going. When He reached the other side of the lake by boat, they were already there waiting for Him.[2]

As Jesus and His disciples now cross the northern border of Palestine for the first time, they arrive in the predominantly gentile region of Tyre and Sidon. He doesn't want anyone to know that He is here.

In Galilee, where He has just been, He found hardly any rest because of all the miracles He did. They drew increasing attention to Him. There were also the Pharisees and teachers of religion who burdened Him with their incessant criticism and endless disputations. Surely no one will follow Him into this gentile country, for it is shunned by the Jews, to whom it is unclean.

Maybe Jesus also desires solitude, in view of His impending death, which is becoming terrifyingly close. On this final trip with His disciples to Jerusalem He may calmly want to prepare them for the hard times ahead.

Whatever the case, the news of Jesus' arrival somehow leaks out. Even on heathen soil He cannot long remain incognito. Right away a mother cries for help. She has a daughter who is demon-possessed. The suffering of such an individual is nearly unbearable, both to herself and to the people immediately around her. And a mother often suffers even more than her child.

This mother has heard that Jesus healed people from Tyre and Sidon when He was in His own land.[3] The news about the man He delivered from a legion of evil spirits has reached her as well.[4] The Lord who has healed so many will not turn her away. Of that she is sure.

"Lord, Son of David, please have mercy on me!" she cries. She so identifies herself with the need of her child that she in fact asks help for herself.

Despite all her pleas and expectations, her appeal doesn't seem to move Jesus. He doesn't say a word. His disciples, feeling no empathy with the woman's need, quickly see this as a refusal. "Send her away," they say. "She keeps crying out after us." To them this individual is invading their rest and privacy. Moreover, a woman—and especially a foreign one—has to be quickly silenced. Her shouts are drawing attention to the Lord, who explicitly wishes to remain unnoticed. Their reaction is harsh, even though it is also prompted by concern for their Master.

Jesus' apparently cool reaction doesn't sprout from a lack of understanding or sympathy with the afflicted woman. His answer proves that. He is simply considering the limitations of His mission. "I was sent only to the lost sheep of Israel."

Jesus does His work in complete dependence on His Father. Doing God's will is meat and drink to Him. The prophets foretold that He, the Messiah, would come first and foremost for His own people. The Word of God has to be spoken to the Jews first.[5] Initially Jesus' mission is to His own country and people.[6] It is the same explicit commission that He has passed on to His disciples.[7]

The Lord has healed non-Jews before, but He has never stepped on foreign soil. The region of Phoenicia or Canaan (presently Lebanon) is not only heathen country. Its inhabitants are also considered archenemies of Israel. Consequently, to Jews this is forbidden territory. Jesus, soon to be rejected by the Jews, knows, however, that He is the Savior of the *world.* Does He therefore wait for an inner affirmation, a sign from God that the door toward the Gentiles is slowly opening now?

Jesus proves again that the Son, loving His heavenly Father, doesn't operate without His approval. His first and utmost desire is to obey God. This even overrules His intense interest in needy people. Jesus refuses to be dictated to by human sorrow, however painful that may prove to be.

To be able to remove sorrow and to reap gratitude and love in return warms Jesus' heart over and again. He has a deep need to be appreciated, just as we do. But in order to obey God He is willing to ignore recognition and to accept misunderstanding. This makes Him extremely vulnerable, and even more lonely. It exemplifies clearly, however, where our priorities should lie.

The woman knows nothing of this. She is captivated by one thought only: I need help for my daughter, and I am not going to be put off. She is determined not to take no for an answer. Her persistence resembles the tenacity of Jacob, who, in a crisis situation, cried out to God, saying, "I will not let you go unless you bless me."[8]

This concerned mother simply states, "Lord, help me!"

Blown and beaten by sorrow, she is at her wit's end. Jesus is her last hope. She is a gentile woman, true, but nevertheless her motivation is something beyond such distinctions: faith. Humbly, respectfully, reverently, she kneels before Jesus, calling Him "Son of David" and "Lord." It is a touching moment, for here across the border Jesus meets the faith that is painfully absent among His own people. Yet His answer is rather perplexing. "It is not right to take the children's bread and toss it to their dogs."

She cannot believe her ears. Why does this great man, who is self-effacing and known for His love for people, give her such a harsh answer? This seems like such a gross contradiction to His invitation, "Come to me, all you who are weary and burdened."[9]

To be rejected, to be compared to a dog—is that being understood? She never felt more gravely insulted!

"Gentile dog" is the name Jews in Jesus' time give to a non-Jew. God has chosen the Jews to be His people. But instead of being humble and thankful for this, they have come to look proudly down on the Gentiles, whom they consider to be unclean dogs.

Maybe Jesus uses this expression in view of His disciples, to verbalize what they think. Their lack of compassion strikes Him painfully. Although they have been moving about with Jesus for a long time, they apparently have learned little from Him in this respect. But Jesus is now about to introduce a new way of thinking. As they move slowly toward Jerusalem, the disciples need to understand that His forthcoming death and resurrection will introduce a new era. Jesus' sacrifice will clearly indicate the end of all prejudices. It will blot out the differences between Jew and Gentile, slave and free, male and female.[10] Just before this incident, Jesus indicated clearly to His disciples that the traditional Jewish difference between clean and unclean food no longer applies. It is not what a person eats but what he thinks that makes him unclean.[11]

The Lord now goes a step further. The distinction between what they call clean and unclean people will also be eliminated. From now on individuals will not be accepted or rejected according to birth or race, but according to *faith*.

Jesus' words sound harsh and puzzling at first, but they don't frighten off the woman. Is she disappointed? She doesn't show it. Sharp-witted, she focuses in on the word Jesus uses for dog. This word doesn't refer to the wandering dogs that scavenge the streets but to the little house pets that, along with the children who love them, belong to the family.

Eating utensils are not yet known. People eat with their fingers. The soiled fingers are wiped off on chunks of bread, which are then flung to the dogs. It is a common practice that the woman knows well.

Her answer is quick and resourceful. "Yes, Lord, yet even the little pups eat the crumbs that fall from their (young) masters' table" (AMP). In other words, she is saying that the Jews enjoy God's grace so abundantly that they won't miss out at all if Gentiles share their blessing. No patient in Palestine will suffer longer just because the Messiah heals my daughter of her demon possession. Helping one doesn't exclude help to the other.

It becomes a play on words between two people who clearly understand one another. This gentile woman understands Jesus better than almost anyone else. She interprets His illustrations according to their true meaning, then picks them up and continues in the same line of thought. She is satisfied to take a secondary place, but she doesn't get sidetracked from the goal for which she came. With a quick mind and a ready wit she confronts the Lord with the implication of His own words. His answer, which seemingly rejects her request, she intelligently turns around as an opening for granting it.

Her culture is not friendly toward women, and her people are certainly not on easy terms with the Jews. Still the woman proves to be relaxed and even bold in her encounter with Jesus. Even the rebuff of the disciples doesn't ruffle her.

The woman senses keenly that in general Jesus is kindly

disposed toward her. She intuits that there are complex fac-
tors of which she has no knowledge that make Him act as He
does. He may challenge her faith but He doesn't want her to
give up. Of that she is certain.

Jesus' reaction to her frank answer is a proof of this.
There is not a touch of disapproval, not a hint that He considers her impertinent or too bold. He doesn't say, "This is not
the way a female talks to a man, and certainly not a gentile
woman to a Jewish rabbi." Any other Jewish man might have
reacted this way. Not Jesus. He appreciates her ready wit. He
regards it positively that she is not to be intimidated. As a
matter of fact, He compliments her for it.

"For such a reply, you may go; the demon has left your
daughter," writes Mark. Matthew adds, "Woman, you have
great faith!" Jesus appreciates faith that doesn't allow itself to
be discouraged. This He illustrates by the parable of a widow
who, in spite of repeated rejection, persistently keeps standing up for her rights. This woman, like this mother, receives
what she desires. Both are examples of faith.[12]

This mother's faith is tried a little longer—until the point
when she arrives at home. Then she sees that her daughter is
truly healed. Who can imagine her joy?

She doesn't know that the incident indicates something
of much broader scope: the opening of a door of salvation to
the Gentiles. The healing of her daughter is the first of many
more miracles to come outside of Palestine.

History repeats itself. Like the Samaritan woman (the first
half-Jew) and later Lydia (the first European),[13] who both
believed, it is again a woman who is privileged to open up a
new door for the spreading of the gospel just beyond the
border of Palestine.

After Jesus' ascension, this incident helps to advance the
cause of expanding missions for the apostles. Twenty years
later, there is a flourishing church in Tyre. In fact, Paul

stays there a week and writes about his touching farewell to one of the first Christian churches.[14]

Are this Canaanite woman and her healed daughter among those who accompany Paul and his colaborers to the ship? Do they kneel with him and the others on the beach to pray? We don't know. But we do know that this region—still often in the news in the twentieth century—reminds us of a woman who wasn't satisfied with a negative answer. It reminds us of a woman who frankly retorted in ready wit, from which she reaped rich fruit.

It is good to think of this gentile woman when we don't receive answers to our prayers right away or when we feel rejected. She stimulates us to be bold in our approach to God, to persevere in praying, and to remember that what seems to be a rejection may prove to be an open door to receive access to God's blessings.

NOTES: 1. Read Matthew 15:21-28 and Mark 7:24-30.
2. Mark 6:30-33
3. Luke 6:17-19
4. Mark 5:1-20
5. Acts 1:8, 13:45-46
6. John 1:11
7. Matthew 10:5-6
8. Genesis 32:26
9. Matthew 11:28
10. Galatians 3:28
11. Matthew 15:10-20
12. Luke 18:1-8
13. Acts 16
14. Acts 21:3-6

QUESTIONS FOR PERSONAL OR GROUP STUDY

1. Consider this woman against the background of the religion of her people. What strikes you in particular about her faith? (1 Kings 11:5-6, 16:31, 18:18, Matthew 11:20-22).

2. Why did she call Jesus "Lord" and "Son of David"? (Matthew 1:1, John 7:40-42).

3. Read Genesis 32:22-28 and Luke 18:1-8 carefully. What similarities do you see in these two passages?

4. Read Genesis 18:20-33. What similarity do you see between Abraham's intercession and the pleading of this gentile woman?

5. Try to visualize yourself in this woman's situation. What would strike you most in the attitude of Jesus and that of His disciples?

6. We cannot go to Jesus face-to-face with our problems. How can we approach Him, however? (Jeremiah 33:3, John 16:24, Philippians 4:6).

7. How do you evaluate the male-female relationship then and now? What kind of influence did Jesus have on this relationship?

8. What is the most important impression this story has left on you?

13
He Esteems Motherhood Highly

"Let the little children come to me, and do not hinder them, for the kingdom of God belongs to such as these."

(Mark 10:14)[1]

Who are the people who come to Jesus with their children? Matthew and Mark leave it undecided. Luke, with a keen eye for human detail, mentions babies. Thus it is generally accepted that we are dealing here with mothers. Although I adopt this theory, since the Bible is not specific I will not exclude fathers. These parents want Jesus to touch their babies, to pray for them and bless them.

In the meantime, the pressure of His impending terrible death is increasingly felt by the Lord. Several times He talks with His disciples about His death, and the resurrection to follow. But the reality of this coming event doesn't penetrate their minds. Even His three best friends are no exception. The first time Jesus mentions it, Peter takes Him aside. "Never, Lord!" he says. "This shall never happen to you!" The Lord then rebukes Peter because rather than speaking the things of God he is speaking as an advocate of the Devil.[2]

When the Lord for the second time plainly talks about His coming suffering, it again makes little or no impression. When right before entering Jerusalem He mentions it again, John and James prove to be more taken up with their own interests than with the imminent suffering of their Master. They cause unrest among the disciples with a question: who among us is the most important? These men who have given up everything apparently still understand very little of what moves Jesus most deeply. They are following after the Lord because they love Him, yet they scarcely understand what motivates Him in His encounters with people.

Just prior to this, Jesus speaks convincingly about how marriage is designed to be sacred and permanent. This is His answer to a question of some Pharisees, who are trying to corner Him as usual. Their attacks still haven't lost any of their caustic edge. It is sad that the leaders of the people don't want to be convinced by Jesus' words and deeds, even at this late hour. More painful than the rejection of the Pharisees, however, is the fact that He is still not being understood by His disciples. These people who are nearest to Him cause Him deep loneliness at a time when He needs their sympathy more than ever.

Then, right after this lecture about marriage, some mothers with their children come to Jesus. It is possible that the mention of marriage gives them the courage to step forward from among the crowd with their children, who are the fruit of marriage.

The act of blessing children has a deep and lasting meaning in Israel. Usually this is done by the fathers. Remember the blessings of the patriarchs Isaac and Jacob to their children and grandchildren, and the lasting influence of those blessings?[3] It is also a Jewish habit for mothers to take their children to an honored rabbi for his blessing on their first birthday. In this way, father and mother are both occupied with the religious education of their children.

Small wonder that these mothers desire that Jesus place His hands upon their children. They have seen the blessed influence of these hands as they remove sickness and pain.

Hands that make the lame and crippled walk and blind people see. They know that with the touch of these hands, dead people return to life. Now, as the Lord visits their region, they won't miss the opportunity to have their children blessed by Him.

But it is difficult to come close to Jesus. You always have to pass His disciples first. This is often an advantage, because the Master sometimes runs the risk of being crushed in a crowd. But the disciples function not as a welcoming committee. On the contrary, they rather look like a brick wall against which the expectations of the mothers could break to pieces. They prove to be resistant when these mothers demonstrate their eagerness for the Lord to bless their children.

Nothing doing! Who do you think you are? the disciples say. The Master has no time. Don't you see how busy He is? He certainly has more important things to do than to busy Himself with small children. These little ones have no idea what it's all about anyway. They can't understand the Master. Move back, all of you! Quickly now. Make way for others who really need the Lord.

True concern for their weary Master certainly has its place. But their disregard for these faithful women and children reveals that the disciples little understand how highly Jesus esteems children. The men don't seem to have learned from the past. Didn't Jesus help a mother with a sick daughter, perhaps just a little older than these children, in the region of Tyre and Sidon? This despite the fact that they wanted to send her away also? Have they forgotten that Jesus neglected their advice then?

Very recently Jesus called a child forward from among the crowds and used him as an object lesson about the Kingdom of Heaven. Don't they remember that warning about not looking down on the little ones?[4]

By now Jesus sees what is going on. Now it is the disciples who are rebuked, not the children.

Jesus is indignant, Mark writes. It is a strong expression that we hardly find elsewhere of the Lord. His indignation is mixed with pain. It startles and grieves the Lord that His closest colaborers, who will soon take over the torch after His departure, have understood so little of His mission. This is the never-ending difficulty from which Jesus suffers His entire lifetime.

The author of Hebrews writes that Jesus "endured . . . opposition from sinful men."[5] Up to a certain extent, this is also the case here. The attitude of the disciples is the opposite of their Master's attitude. (It is thrilling to read how these men change completely after the descent of the Holy Spirit. The letters of Peter and John, for instance, radiate a warmth and understanding we don't see in them before then.)

It is for people that Jesus suffers terribly at the Cross, but this suffering is brief. Jesus' suffering because of people—by bearing with their misunderstanding, rejection, and twisting of His words and motives—lasts His entire life. This also is suffering because of sin. It is difficult for us as human beings to grasp and not to underrate this suffering.

The cool rejection from Israel's religious leaders and the obvious lack of understanding from His disciples is in contrast to the heart-warming attitude of these women. They, by way of exception, come to Jesus not to criticize or to be healed or to be forgiven, but for His blessing. These mothers realize that Jesus is sent by God, that the Holy Spirit dwells in Him. They believe that He has the authority to extend God's blessing upon their children. Therefore they come to Him.

These mothers receive even more than they hoped for. They probably expect Jesus to bless their children together as a group. Jesus does much more. Every baby receives personal attention. The Lord takes each child separately in His arms, puts His hands on the child, and then gives His blessing.

Mothers with children probably remind Jesus of His own mother and all that He owes to her. What is the influence of Jesus' blessing on these little ones as they grow up? It would be interesting to know. No other children have ever felt the touch of the Lord so personally. These become the most privileged babies in the world!

For these mothers (and fathers, if they are present), this experience will always remain to be the most precious memories of their lives, which they will never forget. As their children grow up, they will tell them about this time over and over again.

Jesus' greatest suffering is still ahead of Him: the insults of the Roman authorities, the abuse of the Jewish leaders, the unfaithfulness of His friends. Over these dark hours shines a ray of light because of these mothers and their children.

Along with the many memories the disciples will later cherish about their Lord belongs this brief encounter. They will never forget how Jesus, in spite of the pressure of His last days on earth, showed profound interest in children—even babies. They will continue to remember what He said of them: "Let the little children come to me, and do not hinder them, for the kingdom of God belongs to such as these."

These words are an encouragement to parents today, who, like these mothers then, desire to bring their children to Jesus. They, too, can expect opposition since the ruling opinion today still often underrates motherhood and religious education. For such parents it is good to know that Jesus esteems motherhood highly. He is resentful of people who try to keep children away from Him, even today.

We cannot meet the Lord in person anymore at a specific place or hour. But through prayer He is accessible to all parents who want to have God's blessing on their children. Jesus Himself developed from childhood to adulthood. He did this in relationship to Himself, others, and God. He knows that a child without His blessing will suffer unimaginable and lasting harm. Mothers and fathers, therefore, should take their children to Jesus again and again. In our day they need His blessing more than ever before.

NOTES: 1. Read Matthew 19:13-15, Mark 10:13-16, and Luke 18:15-17.
2. Matthew 16:21-23
3. Genesis 27, Genesis 48
4. Matthew 18:1-10
5. Hebrews 12:3

QUESTIONS FOR PERSONAL OR GROUP STUDY

1. Consider the pain Jesus suffered from the rejection of the Jewish leaders and the misunderstanding of His disciples. How do you think this made Him suffer?

2. How do you think the attitude of the mothers with their children influenced Jesus?

3. In what ways did Jesus develop from childhood through adulthood? (Luke 2:52). Try to think of specific examples.

4. What major differences are there between mothers who raise their children in the things of God and those who don't? (2 Chronicles 22:2-4, 2 Timothy 1:5-6, 3:14-15).

5. What do you learn from the influence of the mothers of Moses (Exodus 2:1-10, Joshua 1:5,7, Psalm 106:23), Samuel (1 Samuel 1:11,27-28, 3:19-21), and John the Baptist (Luke 1:5-7, 57-80)?

6. Think how you could be a better parent to your children.

14
He Entrusts a Woman With a Vital Message

"'Go . . . to my brothers and tell them, "I am return-
ing to my Father and your Father, to my God and
your God."' Mary of Magdala went to the disciples
with the news: 'I have seen the Lord!' And she told
them that he had said these things to her."
(John 20:17-18)[1]

Mary Magdalene is one of the six women named Mary in the New Testament. It is the same name as Miriam in the Old Testament, with the same meaning: bitterness. Like Miriam, the sister of Moses, Mary Magdalene is a remarkable person and a leader of women. Like both Miriam and Mary, the mother of Jesus, she has her share of life's deep troubles. Magdalene means "of Magdala," the area she is from. Magdala is about three miles from Capernaum, a flourishing small industrial town where Jesus often stays.

Mary Magdalene is apparently well off. She can go travel-ing for an indefinite time without needing to earn money. At the same time she gives freely to others from her own resources.

The background, age, and marital status of Mary Magda-lene remain unknown. Most likely she is single. Where she first meets Jesus we don't know. Definitely it is at the end of His second year as an itinerant rabbi, thus over a year before His death.

That meeting causes a radical change in Mary's life, for Jesus cures her of seven evil spirits. Many people in Jesus'

117

time are demon-possessed. Sometimes this plight expresses itself in mental or physical aberrations.[2] How deeply such a person can suffer we see in the man whom Jesus healed from the Gerasenes, which is at the opposite side of the lake from Magdala.[3]

How Mary Magdalene's demon possession expressed itself, we don't know. The fact that there were seven demons, however, reveals that her suffering was severe. Maybe she lacked control over her mental faculties and experienced enormous problems in dealing with both herself and others. Mary Magdalene was thus a hopeless case—until she met Jesus. From that moment on she is free, mentally fit, in harmony with herself and those around her.

Sometimes people whom Jesus heals are ordered to return home to tell about God's goodness. But Mary of Magdala is free to follow Jesus. This she does the rest of her life.

Jesus' life on earth is short. There are but a few who can serve Him unhindered and without interruption. Not many can share His daily burdens with constant dedication. Men and women who have to earn a living and mothers with small children, no matter how much they may want to do this, are excluded. For single people it is easier to follow the Lord. Mary Magdalene has this opportunity and uses it to the full.

Mary supports Jesus out of her own means. She enters into His ministry together with women of more respectable backgrounds, such as Joanna, the wife of Cuza, who was the manager of Herod's household; Salome, the mother of the disciples John and James; and many others. Due to her character and dedication, Mary becomes their leader. This woman with the terrible past becomes a stable personality and a light that shows others the way. When these women are mentioned, her name always appears first.

How these approximately four hundred days of caring for Jesus and His disciples are filled, we do not know. But we do know that Mary Magdalene unintentionally draws attention to herself. It is a small country with primitive forms of communication. There is no press, no radio, no television reporting the miracle-healing of this desperate woman. But the word from mouth to mouth travels quickly. The new, healed Mary Magdalene becomes an attraction who draws people to Jesus.

Naturally there is criticism. There are people who say, "Look at her! Doesn't she remember what she was?" But Mary Magdalene has put her hand to the plow. She refuses to look back, to be slowed down by the past. The new life given to her is purposefully dedicated to the Kingdom of God.[4]

Her gratitude to Jesus for the healing and the privilege of knowing Him reveals itself openly at His death and resurrection. At that time there is a great contrast between her attitude and the disciples' attitude toward Jesus.

As time passes by, Mary Magdalene cannot help but observe the growing opposition and hostility of the religious leaders toward Jesus, culminating in His imprisonment, condemnation, and death. Perhaps she is present that night at the Mount of Olives when Judas hypocritically betrays his Master with a kiss. In the house of the high priest she is shocked to hear Peter deny the Lord three times. Has Peter now forgotten his promise to give his life for Him?

She hears the scornful questions of the Jewish council, which are asked not to discover but to violate the truth. She watches Pilate's cheap gesture when he claims his innocence. Neither the religious nor the worldly authorities are prepared to stand up for Jesus—that is clear.

None of the many lame and crippled people whom Jesus set on their feet spring to His help. None of the mute who can now talk speak up for Him. The thousands who were healed and fed are now painfully absent.

The hysteria of the crowd releases itself at the point

when they are given a choice to free either Jesus or a notorious criminal. Almost unanimously they choose the criminal.

When Jesus is led to the place of the Cross, Mary Magdalene witnesses the greatest crime ever committed. From the
shame of this infamy, no water can ever wash humanity clean.
History records many innocent people being killed, but here
goes a Man whose only crime is that He is and does good. The
paradox of suffering for that gross injustice nobody can
understand, not even Mary Magdalene.

The only ones in the crowded streets of Jerusalem who
express their sorrow are women. Nobody pays attention to
them except Jesus, who always has a keen eye for integrity
and righteousness. There is one woman who tries to save
Jesus' life: the wife of Pilate. This Mary Magdalene doesn't
know.

At the Cross, the personal interest in Jesus has thinned
down to His mother, the women of His team, and John. None
of the other disciples can cope with the pressure. They fail to
come when their Lord needs them most.

Alas, the suffering of the Master still hasn't reached its
lowest point. At the Cross, the symbol of being rejected by the
earth, heaven also proves to be closed to Jesus. The most
painful cry ever uttered comes from Jesus' lips: "My God, my
God, why have you forsaken me?"[5]

The love of Mary Magdalene for her Lord does not end at
His death. Along with some other women, she watches carefully how and where He is buried. Not until there appear
three stars in the firmament, a sign that the Sabbath has
begun, does she go home. That Sabbath day when the body of
the Son of God lies in the grave becomes the saddest day of
her life, and of the history of the world.

The following morning the women are present early at
the grave to embalm Jesus' body. But instead of the dead
body, they find angels, the heralds of Jesus' resurrection.

The angels say to the women, "He is not here; he has risen! Remember how he told you, while he was still with you in Galilee: 'The Son of Man must be delivered into the hands of sinful men, be crucified and on the third day be raised again.'"[6] At this point the women remember. Back in Galilee Jesus told His disciples—and also the women—about His coming suffering and death. He also told them that He would rise on the third day. Both prophecies are now being fulfilled.

"He has risen!" These are the most encouraging words ever spoken. They move the women deeply, although the full extent of the words still escapes them.

Then one of the angels gives the women a commission: "Go, tell his disciples and Peter, 'He is going ahead of you into Galilee. There you will see him, just as he told you.'"[7]

Go and tell. With these words the women are rewarded for their love, faithfulness, and perseverance. They become the first ones to announce Jesus' resurrection. Throughout the centuries many have received their commissions with the same words, but none have ever heard the message so directly.

To the angels and thus to God, whom they serve, from now on the women certainly belong to the group. At the promised meeting in Galilee they are expected. "He is going ahead of you [not only *them,* the disciples] into Galilee. There you [all of you] will see him. . . ."

The women hurry back to the city. Even without the express emphasis to tell the disciples, they would have told them their findings first. After all, they are men whom these women look up to, for whose welfare they have given themselves. The women feel close to them. They have experienced the high and low points of life together. In the past year they have been like family to them. And how happy Peter will be that he is mentioned specifically. There is forgiveness for him.

They find the men in tears and brokenhearted. In spite of this, the reception is like a cold shower. The disciples don't believe a word of what the women are saying! When the initial report of these eyewitnesses doesn't convince them, the women keep talking. They try all their persuasiveness, but to no avail.

Jesus did foretell His resurrection. But somehow this doesn't revive their memories. Heavenly messengers are the source of information. But it leaves no impression. Because the message comes from the mouths of women? Would they believe if men told them?

The disciples know these women well. Over a long period of time they have been able to check daily to make sure that Mary Magdalene's transformation was genuine. These women spent their time, money, and energy for over a year for them. They have *proven* their faithfulness.

Do the disciples forget how Jesus treats women? How He understands and respects them? How without exception He treats men and women as equals?

Imagination! Madness! Nonsense! Women's tales! According to the Jewish prejudice, the disciples consider women incapable of witnessing. They hold themselves in higher esteem. This way of thinking is not based on character or faith—recent experiences certainly leave no room for that—but allegedly on biological differences, their maleness.

Or are there even other issues at stake here? Are these disciples who used to quarrel about rank and position possibly jealous? Is it hard to swallow that women experience a privilege that bypasses them? Every woman can understand how painful this experience must be to Mary Magdalene and the other women. It strikes me that Bible commentators—usually men—overlook this fact. In retrospect, this incident is in a way more painful to these men than to the women. It is they who are confronted with their own negative thinking.

After Jesus' resurrection this incident throws a shadow on their first meeting with Him. The Lord rebukes His disciples for their lack of faith and their stubborn refusal to believe the words of the women.[8]

Peter and John have in the meantime convinced themselves that the grave is indeed empty. But they are not met by angels. Nor does the resurrected Lord reveal Himself to them. That privilege He has reserved for Mary Magdalene, and it is a breathtaking experience indeed.

Again Mary Magdalene receives a message for the disciples, but this time from Jesus Himself. This time the message concerns His impending ascension.

In spite of the fact that Mary Magdalene may be met again by skeptics, the Lord entrusts her with this mission. A woman is chosen to be the first to pass on the words of the Resurrected One. This is the privilege of Mary Magdalene, who through thick and thin has proven how deeply she loves the Lord. Jesus considers Mary Magdalene a capable witness, despite the fact that the Jewish Law was not content with less than two or three witnesses.[9]

Jesus doesn't consider her unworthy just because she is a woman. Nor does He see her against the background of her dubious past. Through her walk with Him after her healing, Mary Magdalene has grown into an intellectually and emotionally balanced woman, able to face problems others run away from. Jesus sees the desire she shares with every woman: to be taken seriously and to shoulder responsibility. That is what He honors.

As the Lord takes leave from His mother, Mary, He entrusts her to the care of John.[10] But no one is asked to be responsible for Mary of Magdala. She has been entrusted with a vitally important commission: "Go and tell!" Jesus takes Mary Magdalene seriously. He gives her a great assignment.

Over her head Jesus speaks to every one of us. No man

should forget and every woman should be aware that at His resurrection Jesus restored woman to her rightful place. It is the place God intended for her from the very beginning.

NOTES: 1. Read Matthew 27:55-61, 28:1-10, Luke 8:1-3, John 19:25-17, and John 20:1-18.
2. Matthew 17:15-18, Mark 9:17-18, Luke 8:27-31
3. Luke 8:26-39
4. Luke 9:62
5. Mark 15:34
6. Luke 24:6-7
7. Mark 16:7
8. Mark 16:14
9. Deuteronomy 19:15, John 8:17
10. John 19:26-27

QUESTIONS FOR PERSONAL OR GROUP STUDY

1. Mary Magdalene was the first person who met the resurrected Lord and who received a message for His disciples. What commission did the Lord Himself later give to His disciples? (Matthew 28:19-20, Mark 16:15, Acts 1:8).

2. Why is it necessary to have a messenger to pass on the gospel? (Romans 10:14-17).

3. According to Paul, what is the essence of the gospel? (1 Corinthians 15:1-4).

4. Mary Magdalene is not the only woman in history whom God entrusted with a mission. What was the task and the influence of Miriam (Exodus 15:20-21, Micah 6:4), Deborah (Judges 4 and 5), and Huldah (2 Chronicles 34:22-28)?

5. What do Mary Magdalene and the other women mentioned in this chapter have to say to you?

6. What mission do you see for women today, and what is your part in it?

APPENDIX

Suggestions for Discussion Groups

Many people have found that the study of Bible characters proves to be very helpful for personal investigation, which is further enhanced by exchanging their findings in a group. For those who want to continue this excellent habit, and for others who want to put this to the test, the following suggestions will be helpful.

PREPARATION FOR A DISCUSSION GROUP

1. Invite people of about the same basic age and interests. In this way you can achieve clearer communication and understanding.
2. A small group of about six people is ideal. If there are more than ten who wish to participate, form a second group. In this way the number is large enough for profitable discussion but small enough for everyone to join in.
3. Discuss beforehand how often you wish to meet. Start, for instance, with four to six times. Since each chapter of this book forms a complete study within itself, you can choose chapters that are of most interest to you. After meeting a

few times, you can decide if you wish to continue, and for how long.

4. Ask each participant to purchase a copy of the book, to study the chapter to be discussed, and to answer the questions at home beforehand. This will assure that the discussion is the result of personal study. You will also have less trouble sticking to the subject.

5. Encourage all group members to do their utmost to attend each meeting.

6. Meet in a pleasant atmosphere. Be sure the room is well ventilated and the temperature comfortable. If it is too warm or too cool, people will not be at ease. Also be sure that no one has to look into a bright light. The success of your discussion often depends on details like these.

7. Plan the seating arrangement ahead of time. It might be best to sit in a circle. Plan any other details carefully so that you can begin and end on time.

PERSONAL PREPARATION FOR THE LEADER

1. Pray for yourself and for each member of the group. Pray that Christ will speak through His Word to every person present. Ask the Holy Spirit to make you sensitive to the needs of the people in your group.

2. Consider yourself a regular member of the group, but one whose task it is to see that all points of the study are discussed and that the discussion proceeds pleasantly.

3. Be sure you spend sufficient time doing the study yourself. Since questions are already given at the end of each chapter, it should not be too difficult to lead a discussion.

4. As you prepare, consider which points you wish to emphasize. Put those points before the group in the form of questions that stimulate thinking, that can be answered from the Scriptures, and that apply to practical daily living.

Avoid questions that can be answered with a simple yes or no. Good questions often begin with the words *who, what, where, why,* and *how.*

5. Summarize each point that is discussed, or have someone in the group do so before going on to the next question.
6. Although group members can take turns leading, it is good for the same person to do it a number of times in order to get experience.

DURING THE DISCUSSION

1. Maintain a relaxed, informal atmosphere that allows people to get to know one another.
2. Consider each question for its own value. Some will require only a short answer, while others will need to be enlarged upon.
3. Keep the questions general. If you do direct a specific question to an individual for a particular reason, be sure you have that person's permission to do so ahead of time.
4. Allow sufficient time for those in the group to answer. Do not be afraid of silences. If necessary, repeat the question in a natural and easy manner.
5. The ideal discussion group interacts like
   this: not like this:

6. Help the shy people in the group participate. For instance, have them read the question or appropriate verse aloud. People who talk easily in a group sometimes have to be restrained or they will dominate the discussion.

7. Demonstrate that each person is making a valid contribution. Show that you appreciate each contribution, whether or not it is to the point. If the answer is wrong, then ask, "What do others think?"

8. If a question is asked by someone in the group, let others attempt to answer it before you do. The leader of the group shouldn't dominate either!

9. If desired, you can use part of the discussion time for praying together. However, this should be done with tact. If some would rather not, don't pray as a group until a later time when they do want to have group prayer.

10. Keep your objective of changed lives in view. Your goal is not just to increase in knowledge, but to apply God's Word and its principles to daily living.

POSSIBLE TIME ARRANGEMENT OF A DISCUSSION GROUP

1. First get-together:

fifteen minutes	arrival; refreshments
one hour	getting acquainted
one-half hour	deciding future plans

2. The next get-togethers:

fifteen minutes	arrival; refreshments
ten minutes	review
one hour	discussion
twenty minutes	finishing up; next assignment; possibly group prayer

Bibliography

Barclay, William, *The Daily Study Bible*. Edinburgh, Scotland: The Saint Andrew Press, 1983.

Belben, Howard, *The Mission of Jesus*. Colorado Springs: NavPress, 1985.

Bavinck, J. and Edelkoort, A.H., *Bijbel met verklarende kanttekeningen*. Baarn, The Netherlands: Bosch & Keuning N.V., 1954.

Brooks, Pat, *Daughters of The King*. Carol Stream, Illinois: Creation House, 1975.

Halley, Henry H., *Halley's Bible Handbook*. Grand Rapids: Zondervan, 1962.

Hendricks, Jeanne, *A Woman for All Seasons*. Nashville, Tennessee: Thomas Nelson, Inc., 1977.

Henry, Matthew, *Verklaring van het Nieuwe Testament*. Kampen, The Netherlands: J.H. Kok, 1910.

Herr, Ethel L., *Chosen Women of the Bible*. Chicago: Moody Press, 1976.

Jager, Okke, *Opklaring*. Ede, The Netherlands: Zomer & Keuning, 1981.

Karssen, Gien, *Her Name Is Woman* (1 & 2). Colorado Springs: NavPress, 1975, 1977.

Ketter, Peter, *Christus en de vrouwen*. Hilversum, The Netherlands: N.V. Paul Brand's Uitg. Bedrijf, 1937.

Kuyper, A., *Vrouwen uit de Heilige Schrift*. Kampen, The Netherlands: J.H. Kok N.V.

Lockyer, Herbert, *All the Apostles of the Bible*. London: Picker-
  ing & Inglis Ltd., 1975.

Lockyer, *The Women of the Bible*. 1969.

Lockyer, *Wat Jezus leerde over . . . vrouwen. . . .* Hoornaar,
  The Netherlands: Gideon, 1976.

Modersohn, Ernst, *Die Frauen des Neuen Testaments*.
  Neuhausen-Stuttgart, Germany: Hänssler Verlag, 1972.

Moor-Rignalda, A.M. de, *Vrouwen als u en ik*. Kampen, The
  Netherlands: J.H. Kok N.V.

Morton, H.V., *Women of the Bible*. London: Methuen & Co.
  Ltd., 1941.

Nagy, Akos, *Siehe, ich bin des Herrn Magd*. Uhldingen/See-
  wis, Germany: Stephanus Edition, 1979.

National Geographic Society, *Life in Bible Times*. Washington,
  D.C., 1968.

Ockenga, Harold J., *Women Who Made Bible History*. Grand
  Rapids: Zondervan, 1976.

Pape, Dorothy R., *In Search of God's Ideal Woman*. Downers
  Grove, Illinois: InterVarsity, 1976.

Price, Eugenia, *God Speaks to Women Today*. Grand Rapids:
  Zondervan, 1964.

Price, *The Unique World of Women*. 1970.

Sayers, Dorothy L., *Are Women Human?* Grand Rapids: Wm.
  B. Eerdmans, 1974.

Tenney, Merrill C., ed., *The Pictorial Encyclopedia of the
  Bible*. Grand Rapids: Zondervan, 1975.

Tournier, Paul, *The Gift of Feeling*. London: SCM Press Ltd.,
  1982.

Vander Velde, Frances, *She Shall Be Called Woman*. Grand
  Rapids: Kregel Publications, 1977.

Wahlberg, Rachel Conrad, *Jesus According to a Woman*. New
  York: Paulist Press, 1975.

Whyte, Alexander, *Bible Characters*. London: Oliphants Ltd.,
  1967.